YO-ABL-361

WINNING

OR LOSING

WINNING *OR*
LOSING
THE **FINANCIAL &**
RETIREMENT *RACE*

ROBERT D. LAMOREAUX, JD
AUTHOR OF
ESTATE PLANNING MADE E-Z

DEVERE PUBLISHING

OREM, UTAH

ISBN 978-0-9787988-0-2
ISBN 0-9787988-0-5

Library of Congress Control Number:
        2006906685

Published by Devere Publishing, Inc. PO Box 970965, Orem, UT.
        84097-0965
Printed in the U.S.

Visit our websites:
        winningorlosing.com
        deverepublishing.com

Edited by: Don E. Norton Jr.

Photos:
        Summerill Photography, summphoto.com
        LCJ Photography

This book is dedicated to Pegs, without whose support

and encouragemant it would not have been possible,

and to my best fourteen teachers.

Preface

Early in my career, I realized that financial, estate and retirement planning was something that everyone needed. Everyone was going to get older, and hopefully retire, and like birth, all were going to pass away. I also realized that very few people were prepared for death or retirement, and most were not financially prepared for any of the contingencies which come from these events. I found that most people were unprepared for these events and it became my goal to prepare as many as possible for these future events.

How to proceed, I did not know, but proceed I must. I started to obtain more education, only to find that what was needed was a method to disseminate the information to more people. The answer to this question continued to elude me. I traveled, gave seminars in banks, senior citizen groups, church groups and corporations. Although these efforts produced some results, they did not achieve the level of instruction for the general population that I wanted.

In 1991 I copyrighted my first book, *Estate Planning Made E-Z.* I hoped this book, which was complete, along with forms for trusts and wills, would get to enough people that it would start to make a difference. Although the idea was ahead of its time, it still did not accomplish my desire to prepare more people for the future.

In 2004 while attending the 49th annual Estate Planning Seminar in Seattle, Washington, I sat one evening pondering the problem which had eluded me for over thirty years: "How do I get this important information to as many people as possible, as inexpensively as possible, and as soon as possible?" This book is the answer to that question.

Included in this book is the information I know best. It is the culmination of over 35 years of experience. I have not tried to answer all the questions, but have tried to focus on things your professional normally does not tell you. Most often your professional will say, "Let's do this or that" without telling you why— just do it. I wanted to give you, the reader, information with which to make good choices. I wanted you, the reader, to think about why you were doing the things you do—why this financial institution, why this attorney, why this insurance, why this child, why this retirement plan, or why not these things?

This life is a race, and we are all headed toward the finish line faster than we can prepare. Accidents, poor health, disabilities, layoffs, natural disasters and a hundred other things are on the raceway. Any one of these things can, and will, end the race. If an individual is not prepared, the results can be disastrous for you or the survivors. My hope is that what is contained herein will be of benefit to you and your family. It is my desire that you finish the race of life in grand style, cheered on by those around you. Good luck.

TABLE OF CONTENTS

INTRODUCTION

INTRODUCTION

Each individual is a key runner in the race for financial success and quality of life. We run this race because we have no other choice—we are alive. Everybody in the world runs the race, but we have a better running field in the United States. Failure to run the race or follow the rules will result in financial disaster, which will affect one's physical and mental health, and can result in severe suffering and premature death. This race of life is subtle and has complex rules, which vary for each individual; and only after many years can it be determined if we win or if we lose.

After thirty-five years of doing estate planning, I've learned a few rules of the race which I believe can benefit all who will listen and understand. I don't pretend to be the ultimate expert in all things, nor do I believe I have the answers to all the questions. This is not a legal treatise that will teach you all the in's and out's of the law. Many professionals can respond to those needs for you. However, I do believe that much good can come from positive advice concerning the rules of the race that leads to retirement.

We all seek the good life and a long and prosperous retirement, but the facts don't support that hope. I have seen poor health, loss of loved ones, broken finances, and broken homes. Much of this pain and suffering is caused by two major issues: first, lack of knowledge; and second, lack of timely planning. This book addresses both issues in-depth so that readers will, if they have the desire and the guts to do something about it, have a better retirement, and win the race.

Retirement is so intimately associated with financial planning, estate planning and taxes that I include materials from all these areas. Retirement without all of these matters in proper order could result in a disaster. You may lose the race.

I'll address these subjects to four different readers:

First, to the young who are just getting started, those who have time to direct their destiny, those who, if they act in their younger years, can enjoy the long and prosperous retirement.

Second, to those who are half-way there, those who have only thought about retirement, but know it is far off, who have not yet acted, who can still change the course of their future. They may, in many cases, find planning painful, but they still have time to avoid much of the regret in retirement.

Third, to those who are staring retirement in the face, or who have already partaken of retirement and now hope somehow to hold on; those who hope to stay healthy, who hope to not lose all their money, who hope that insurance costs don't go up, that the car continues to work, that prices don't rise, that Social Security continues, and that the *golden* years are really golden.

Fourth, I've thrown in a few pointers which those of any age or situation may use to make this race of life better.

This book does not contain all the information about rules, regulations and laws pertaining to financial, estate and retirement planning. Only volumes could accomplish that task. The law is so complex that with failure to get the right type of help, one can expect bad results and loss of money. This book provides information that, if considered, will ease the stress of going into retirement. If you start early enough, you may be able to improve your financial situation in retirement.

As you read, remember that this book is only a tool to help you plan your race for retirement. Use it as a workbook. If you find any section helpful, take notes for future reference.

CHAPTER ONE

SET THE RULES

Every race has rules to run by and a method for timing. If you do not keep time, how will you know if you are winning? This chapter establishes some basic rules that will allow you to determine if you are winning or losing the race.

AGE OF RETIREMENT

Almost every time I speak with young people and ask them at what age they want to retire, the answer is around 45 to 50, and they all want to be millionaires. That may be a worthwhile goal, but most will not reach it. However, the younger you are when you start implementing your plan, the better chance you will have to achieve your goal.

Retirement is a function of how much money you have, not how old you are. Retirement also means different things to different people. Some people, when they retire, don't go to work regularly but continue to be very productive for many years. Some sit on the couch and watch TV, some fish and hunt, some travel, some spend time with family and become involved in the lives of other people. Whatever your vision of retirement might be, your goal must be to have enough assets (money) to enable you to live the lifestyle you want. When you have acquired that amount of money through your efforts and investments, then you can retire.

1

For retirement, too many people depend on when they can qualify for Social Security and Medicare insurance. These are poor factors to determine when you can retire. Ideally, if you plan ahead and carry out your plan, you can retire before you qualify for Social Security, and when Social Security comes, you can put it all into investments.

NOTES TO SELF

_____

_____

NET WORTH

When I meet with someone to do their estate planning, I always ask, "What is your net worth?" Most people do not have an answer. I find that young people, just out of college, generally have a negative net worth—they owe more than they have. The goal in life is to increase your net worth as quickly as possible so that when you reach retirement, you have sufficient assets to maintain yourself through the retirement stage of life. When you reach retirement age, if you have not accumulated enough assets to support you through retirement, you will either have to decrease your standard of living or continue working. It's all a function of your net worth.

The Net Worth chart at the end of this chapter (Chart #1) is one I have used to determine a person's net worth. It is a simple form, but it will give you a fairly good idea of where you stand. There are many forms to do this, some very complex, but it is essential that you know where you stand at the present time, where you must be at retirement, and what you must do to get there.

When you know where you are financially, you can use a budget to plan your retirement. These two tools, budget and net worth, when used on a regular basis, will help you achieve your goals. It has been said, "Failure to plan is a plan to fail." If you don't know where you are going financially or how you are going to get there, you won't arrive at where you want to be, only where you are headed.

NOTES TO SELF

CASH FLOW

I have always said that cash flow is everything. Every business survives on cash flow. If there is no cash flow, the business dies. The next important thing to know about cash flow is how much of it you keep. To a business this is called profits. To most Americans, this is discretionary income. That means you can spend it how you want. It is how you spend the discretionary funds that determines what type of retirement you will have.

The average individual obtains cash flow from a job. What you do with your cash can be determined by filling out the Cash Flow Chart which appears at the end of this chapter (Chart #2). Once you know where your cash is going, you can determine how much your discretionary income is. It is what you do with the discretionary income that will determine the quality of your retirement. If you are wise enough to invest these discretionary amounts regularly, over a long period of time, in wise investments, your retirement can maintain your present life style and provide for all of your unforeseen needs in the future. There are many good forms for determining cash flow. The cash flow chart included at the end of this chapter will answer most of the important questions about where your income is coming from and where it is going.

When you have filled out your cash flow statement correctly, you can prepare a budget to control expenditure and investments.

You must have cash flow, for without cash flow, you will be stuck on government programs that care for the poor and needy. These programs take away all of a person's dignity. You will be stuck with a Medicare program, which is mediocre at best, and you will wait for others to bring you a Thanksgiving turkey, because you will not be able to afford one. *Cash flow is everything.*

NOTES TO SELF

_____

_____

BUDGET

You must have a *budget*. I'm always amazed at how many people don't know how much they make or where it goes. When I ask if a person has a budget, the answer generally is, "No, but I know where the money goes and I'm always broke." The "always broke" is the direct result of not having a budget and not tracking income and expenses. I recently met an individual who said, "I just can't make it, and I don't know why." When we put together a cash flow statement, his expenses per month were $3,925.00, his income was $2,750.00, yet he didn't understand why he had lost his home

.

In preparation for retirement you must begin at a young age to budget your money. You must know where it is coming from and where it is going. By the time you reach retirement, you must answer the same questions to determine if you can retire. After you retire, you must know where your money is coming from and where it is going. Failure to budget your money at any stage in your life can result in financial disaster.

The Budget Chart which appears at the end of this chapter (Chart #3) will allow you to track your monthly expenditures. When you develop the ability to stay within your budget, you are on your way to a better retirement. Failure to stay within a budget indicates that something is wrong and needs to be corrected. The correct use of a budget should result in a positive cash flow. The excess cash, over budgeted needs, should be invested for retirement.

When you budget your money properly, several important things will happen in your life:

- You will not spend your money on frivolous items.
- You will not spend more than you have coming in.
- You will know how much discretionary income you have for your investments.
- You will know if you can afford a new car or a used one.
- You will understand the hidden costs of owning a home and buying a car, such as taxes, insurance, gas and oil.

You must have a budget and you must keep it up to date. Most important, you must live within that budget, and you must do so your entire life.

NOTES TO SELF

_____

_____

TIME

This book has been written with a view toward things you need to know about retirement. As a result, most people who buy this book are more mature (a ten-dollar word for *older*). But for those who are younger and fortunate enough to purchase this book and put into practice the fundamental philosophy included herein, they will be better prepared and able to move into retirement sooner than those who start later in life. Of all the fancy words used when we talk about qualified plans, pensions, investments and life and health insurances, the concept I think most important for you to understand is the *time value of money.* This concept has to do with the return a person receives on investments over a period of time. The concept is quite simple: *The longer you have an investment, the greater will be the return on that investment.* Let me illustrate:

If $10,000 is invested at 6% for ten years, you will have $17,908 at the end of the ten-year period. If you invest $10,000 at 6% for twenty years, you will have $32,071. If you invest $10,000 at 6% for thirty years, you will have $57,435. If you invest $10,000 at 6% for forty years, you will have $102,857. Note that the total of four times the $17,908 received the first ten years is $71,632, which is $31,255 less than the amount received when the investment is left for forty years. The difference is the value of your compound interest when the investment is left over a period of time.

Date	Annual Interest Rate	Deposit Amount	Interest Paid	Account Value
Jan. 07	6,000	10,000	------	--------
10 years	6,000	0	7,908	17,908
20 years	6,000	0	22,071	32,071
30 years	6,000	0	47,435	57,435
40 years	6,000	0	92,857	102,857

The result is much the same when you amortize a regular investment. As charted out below, you will note that the interest received in the later years of an investment is much higher than in the beginning years. For example, when you put $500.00 dollars per month into an investment at 6%, the interest earned on your investment for the first year is $199.00. The interest earned in the last year of this ten-year investment is $4,623.00, which is $4,424.00 more than you received in the first year. See the chart below.

Date		Deposits	Total Deposits	Interest	Account Value
Jan.	06	6,000	6,000	199	6.199
Jan.	07	6,000	12,000	581	12,780
Jan.	08	6,000	18,000	987	19,766
Jan.	09	6,000	24,000	1,418	27,184
Jan.	10	6,000	30,000	1,875	35,059
Jan.	11	6,000	36,000	2,361	43,420
Jan.	12	6,000	42,000	2,877	52,297
Jan.	13	6,000	48,000	3,424	61,721
Jan.	14	6,000	54,000	4,005	71,727
Jan.	15	6,000	60,000	4,623	82,349

The point of this entire exercise is to impress upon you the fact that the earlier you can start investing for retirement, the better off you will be. The twenty-year-old who can control his or her spending habits and invest regularly toward retirement will be able to accumulate large amounts of money. Those who wait until the later years to start preparing for retirement simply do not have time to accumulate large investments. Start now, wherever you are, to invest toward retirement. Those who say, "I will start tomorrow," must realize that tomorrow never comes; it is always sometime in the future. Time is neither friend nor foe, it is a tool to be used with discretion; and once it is gone, it can never be regained. I believe the goals listed below are the most important to start with:

NOTES TO SELF

_____

_____

GOALS

Several years ago, I took the family on a vacation in the motor home. Our goal was to visit Niagara Falls, New York City, the Boardwalk in New Jersey, Philadelphia, Washington DC, Cary, North Carolina, Cumberland Gap, and Mammoth Cave in Kentucky. Once we had set this goal, it took a lot of preparation to complete the trip. Had we not had the goals, we might have become lost in Nebraska. Goals are absolutely essential to achieve any worthy accomplishment. Some goals will especially improve one's quality of life in retirement.

- An important goal is to obtain as much *education* as possible in whatever area you choose. Education opens the door to more income, a better life style, better family relations, and better retirement. In fact, even after retirement, you need to continue to read and study and educate yourself in many areas. This process will help keep you young.

- You must have goals for your *family*. I believe that the family is everything; nothing else counts in life. When you are dead and gone, everything you acquire in this life will stay behind. All the *stuff* of value to you will have little value to others. The only thing you will take with you is your family relationships. I believe you should use most of your time in setting and pursuing family goals.

- Most, if not all, of our goals in life depend on our financial ability to achieve them. Education costs money, vacations cost money, families cost money (children are expensive), homes cost money, retirement costs money, and health care costs money. All these things are determined by your financial health. Your *financial* goals will involve every phase of your life. They may

8

change from time to time, but they must be pursued with the tenacity of an Olympic long-distance runner.

There are many professionals who can help you set and achieve your goals, whether the goals be educational, financial, family, religious, charitable or retirement. Seek out competent professionals in the areas that are most important to you. Set your goals, work at them, pursue them, don't give up on them, and make them your life, for whatever goals you set will determine what your life will be.

A final word on goals. It is imperative that you make all your goals with your spouse. If only one of you is working toward the goals, it will not work. You must make the goals together and work on them together. One of the most difficult things for a surviving spouse to accomplish is to put everything in order after the death of a spouse, especially if the deceased spouse handled all the finances, pursued all the goals and took all the information with him or her when he or she died. Goals and financial maters must be written and shared with the spouse.

NOTES TO SELF

_____

_____

FINANCIAL OR LEGAL ADVICE

I once met an old rancher who had a lot of property but not much money. The estate was quite large, and because he lived in a very dry area, his water shares were worth a great deal of money. After completing the Trust and during the time we were transferring his assets into the Trust, he called to inform me that his shares of water stock could not be transferred into the Trust. When I asked him why he thought they could not be transferred, he said, "When I was having coffee with the boys at the café this morning, they told me it couldn't be done." On another occasion, a client informed me he didn't want a Trust because the postman said Trusts were illegal. If people have never been successful in these areas, why should we be so gullible as to accept their uneducated opinions? Why is it that broke people so quickly offer advice on legal and financial matters?

America enjoys the greatest financial success of any nation in the world. There never has been, and probably never will be, a nation that has accomplished so much for the benefit of humankind in such a short period of time. We have, in this nation, the best trained financial advisers, attorneys, investment advisers, insurance personnel and retirement personnel of any nation in the world. These professionals are here and are available for you to use and benefit from their knowledge. It is my recommendation that when you need assistance in financial or legal matters, you seek out a professional in your area to help you. These professionals are well trained, and if you follow the guidelines for finding a professional that I have expressed below, they will be of great benefit to you in financial matters. However, if you accept advice on critical items from the guys down at the coffee shop, you deserve what you get. Remember, what you get for nothing isn't worth what you pay for it.

NOTES TO SELF

SELECTING YOUR PROFESSIONALS

I have watched for many years the professionals with whom I have associated. Some are very good in their area of expertise, and some are mediocre to lacking. I believe it is important for you to have the best. Therefore, I offer the following guidelines when choosing a professional, whether it be an attorney, CPA, financial planner, insurance person, or stockbroker:

- Don't pick someone who is new in the industry. They are just learning, and you don't want them to learn at your expense.

- Don't pick someone who is really old, way over retirement age. They may know a lot, but usually are just coasting and not keeping up with changes.

- Do not pick someone who is practicing by themselves or is a sole practitioner, unless they specialize in your specific area of need. They can't do it all.

- Pick someone who is a specialist in the area in which you are seeking counsel.

11

- Choose an insurance person who is affiliated with a major company, one that will be there when you need it, a company with good ratings.

- Choose a CPA, not an accountant, and get one that deals with taxes on a regular basis. One who does not, cannot keep up with the changes in the tax laws.

- Select an attorney from a medium to large law firm who specializes in financial or estate planning.

- Select a financial advisor you can trust, one who will teach you about all the *charges and fees*. You don't want to get one that charges you a fee every year just to *manage your account*.

- Select an advisor who will meet with you annually to review where you are and what changes need to be made to get you where you want to go.

- Go to the professional's office. You can tell a lot about the person by observing his or her surroundings

It is also important to know that you can fire your professional. He or she is the employee. You are paying him or her, and if he or she isn't doing the job, isn't listening, isn't moving and completing your work, isn't nice, is ugly, or for any other reason that may be bothering you, get rid of him or her and get another.

Chart #1 - NET WORTH

Assets

Residence	$
Furnishings	$
Automobiles	$
Other real estate	$
Art, jewelry, or other valuables	$
Cash	$
Checking	$
Savings	$
Stocks	$
Mutual funds	$
Life insurance cash value	$
401 K	$
IRA	$
Notes and trust deeds.	$
Total Assets	**$**

Liabilities

Home mortgage	$
Other mortgage	$
Automobile loans	$
Bank loans	$
Personal loans	$
Credit card	$
Other debts	$
Total Liabilities	**$**

Net Worth

Total assets	$
Total liabilities	$
Net Worth (subtract your liabilities from your assets)	**$**

13

Chart #2 - CASH FLOW

Mortgage payment or rent	$	Automobile expenses (gas, repairs, etc.)	$
Automobile loan(s)	$	Life insurance	$
Personal loans	$	Homeowner's insurance	$
Charge accounts	$	Automobile insurance	$
Withholding and taxes	$	Health insurance	$
IRA	$	Medical expenses	$
401(k)	$	Entertainment/dining	$
Real estate taxes	$	Recreation/travel	$
Utilities (electricity, heat, water, telephone, etc.)	$	Club dues	$
Credit cards	$	Gifts	$
Food	$	Professional services	$
Clothing/laundry	$	Charitable contributions	$
Education	$	Other expenses	$
Child care	$	**Total Expense**	**$**

Monthly Income

Wages, salary, tips	$
Alimony, child support	$
Dividends from stocks, mutual funds, etc.	$
Interest on savings accounts, bonds, CDs, etc.	$
Social Security benefits	$
Pensions	$
Other income	$
Total Monthly Income	**$**

Net Cash Flow

Total Monthly income	$
Total monthly expenses	$
Discretionary monthly income (subtract your expenses from your income)	**$**

NOTE: Discretionary income shows how much you have left to invest.

Chart #3 - BUDGET

MONTH

Mortgage payment or rent		Automobile expenses (gas, repairs, etc.)	
Automobile loan(s)		Life insurance	
Personal loans		Homeowner's insurance	
Charge accounts		Automobile insurance	
Withholding and taxes		Health insurance	
IRA		Medical expenses	
401(k)		Entertainment/dining	
Real estate taxes		Recreation/travel	
Utilities (electricity, heat, water, telephone, etc.)		Club dues	
Credit cards		Gifts	
Food		Professional services	
Clothing/laundry		Charitable contributions	
Education		Other expenses	
Child care		**Total**	

Every month, you should check to see if the amount spent exceeds or is less than the planned budget. If there are excess expenses, you must change something to make it work.

NOTES TO SELF

_____

_____

_____

CHAPTER TWO

MONEY MANAGEMENT

SELECT A STRATEGY

The strategy of your race must involve your attitude toward money—how to make it and how to keep it. There are many options to select from. The following suggestions are only a beginning. When additional items arise, if they are consistent with those already selected, you will have a strong foundation for running the race.

MONEY

There are probably as many approaches to money as there are people. These range from those who worship money to those who hate money. From the penthouse to the hermitage, from the large estate to the mud hut, each has his or her own vision as to what money means. Money, like all other things, is a tool to be used to accomplish goals in life. Having given much thought to this, I have reduced my philosophy on money to a few small items which, to me, seem very important.

- Money is a tool—nothing more, nothing less. It helps accomplish goals and dreams.
- It is not how much money you make that counts, it is how much money you keep.
- Having money sooner is better than later. The longer the

time period you have money, the more things you can do with it.

- More money is better than less money. More money buys you more options, it reaches more goals, and it buys you a better retirement.
- Money allows you to benefit your church, give to charity, and bless many individual lives.

Money is absolutely an essential part of life—you can't escape it, and you can't live without it. When you reach retirement, your quality of retirement will depend on how much you made and what you did with it. Your attitude toward the money you receive will determine the happiness of yourself and those around you.

NOTES TO SELF

_____

_____

GET RICH QUICK

As we mature and get closer to retirement, particularly past the age of fifty, we tend to look at where we are financially and panic. Either we go into depression, or we react in such a manner as to further complicate our financial stability by making bad investments. Friends will regularly inform you of *so and so* who invested in *this or that* and made a great haul. The fact of the matter is, in almost every instance, when you invest on a *great deal*, the deal isn't so great, and you lose money.

There are no great *GET RICH QUICK* schemes. There are those who make money on these programs, but most of them are already in prison or should be in prison. The fact is that the regular guy who is getting ready for retirement is almost always the loser.

The closer you get to retirement, the less time you have to recover your investment if you lose money. When you are 20 and you lose $10,000 in an investment, you have 45 years to recover that $10,000. When you are 60 years old and you lose $10,000, you only have 5 years to recover that investment. When you are 70 years old and lose $10,000, you have no time to recover that investment. It is gone forever. Thus the older you get, the more conservative you should be in your investments.

What is a safe rate of return for you as you approach retirement? This amount changes with the economy, but if the going interest rate is four (4%) percent and someone promises you a twenty (20%) percent rate of return or higher, does that not seem unrealistic? Anytime a person promises more than five (5%) percent above the going rates of return, it is extremely risky, and you should not enter such a transaction without consulting with your legal and financial advisors. *Remember: If it sounds too good to be true, it usually is!*

NOTES TO SELF

_____

_____

DEBT

One of the biggest hindrances to our ability to retire is debt. We live in a society where debt is fostered, encouraged, and almost forced upon an individual. You can buy almost anything and finance it in countless ways. It all adds up to huge amounts of debt. Debt in any form can keep you from retiring, can stifle your ability to invest and save, can deter you from travel, and can destroy your physical, emotional and mental health. When you are ready to retire, you must be out of debt. Your home must be paid for, your car must be paid for, and you must have a zero balance due on your credit cards.

There are things in life for which one must generally go in debt to acquire. Few people have the ability to buy a home with cash. It is an item we must finance. When financing a home, get the best interest rate you can negotiate, and a fifteen-year payoff. Your financial advisor can show you the benefits of this arrangement, which add up to tens of thousands and maybe hundreds of thousands of dollars in savings to you. It is imperative, however, that your home be free and clear before you retire.

Sometimes you will need to finance a car, but buying a year-old model may save you ten thousand dollars. It is not necessary to buy a new car every year. Wear the car out—drive it 250 thousand miles, get your money out of it. If you take care of your car, it will look good and run well for a long time. Remember, it is a tool, not a personality. It is only a car.

Many times you are required to go into debt to obtain an education for your chosen profession or skill. The cost of education keeps going up, and for many families it is impossible to save enough money to educate all the children. I believe an education is essential for young people in our society today, and they must do whatever they can to obtain an education, even if it involves going into debt. One option is to borrow the money through student loans. In my day, I worked full-time while going through school, and I believe students today should work at least part-time to help pay for their education. If they obtain an education without putting something into it themselves, it won't mean as much to them. It is like giving children a car and a credit card: if they don't pay for the car, the gas, and insurance, they don't take care of it. But if they pay for the car, the gas, and insurance, they will treat it with much more respect.

WANTS & NEEDS

Many things in life may require financing, but our society would have you lose control of those decisions. Everyone wants to sell you something and will arrange financing; and without some restraints, bankruptcy lurks right around the corner. I believe you must draw a strict line between wants and needs. Most salespersons would have you believe you *need* whatever they are selling. I want a new car, but do I need one? No, this car is still running fine! I want a trip to Disneyland, but do I need one? No, I can live without it! I want a new television, but do I need one? No, the color and picture of this one are still good.

In order to control your debt, you must determine weather you *want* the item or *need* the item. If it is a need, then save your money and get it when you have the cash. If it is a want, then save your money and get it when your needs have been met. In almost all instances, whether it be a want or a need, you have the time and ability, when you exercise some self-control, to buy the items with cash. When you buy a $500 television set at 10% interest over a two-year period, the television set actually costs over $600. When you save the money at 10% interest over a two-year period to buy the television set, it costs you about $470 dollars, because your savings paid interest. The net result is a savings of over $130. The results are even larger at higher interest rates. When you apply this principle to all the things you buy in your life, the net result is a lot of money in your retirement fund when you retire. Remember, retirement doesn't depend on age, it depends on how much money you have.

CREDIT CARDS

The most financially destructive institution in our society is the credit card, available from almost every financial institution in our nation. You may receive applications in the mail at the rate of five to ten a month. Many times, issuance of the card is automatic. Almost anyone can qualify. I have a friend who has a credit card for his dog and his cat, both qualified, with little or no income. Although a credit card may make shopping and travel very convenient, the problem comes from people not being able to manage credit cards. We get caught in the present-day philosophy of *I need it now, and I can pay for it later.* I personally am considered by many to be old-fashioned and out of touch with financial reality, but I believe a credit card should be used only when absolutely necessary and should be paid in full every month. The trap most people fall into is using many cards for many purchases and ultimately not being able to pay all the bills from all the credit cards.

A $10,000 credit card debt at 18% costs you $1,800 dollars in interest annually. If you pay $150 dollars a month, you never pay off the bill, you only pay the interest. Over a six-year period you have paid $10,800 in interest and you still owe the $10,000. How smart is that? If you put $150.00 dollars a month away at 18% for six years you will have over $19,200 dollars. Which do you prefer—$10,000 debt over the six years or $19,000 dollars in your investment? (You can't get 18% safely today in an investment, but you can sure pay it when you borrow the money.) If you cannot control your credit card and pay it off monthly, get rid of it. If you are already caught in the bind and have high credit card debt, cut the cards up and do not use them anymore. Do you now understand how I feel about credit cards? Many retirements are destroyed by credit cards, either before or after retirement.

NOTES TO SELF

_____

_____

DEBIT CARDS

Debit cards look like credit cards, smell like credit cards, and are accepted like credit cards, but they are generally not credit cards. A debit card is an electronic check which, when used, deducts the payment directly from your checking account. The use of the card is very convenient, and it is accepted by almost every business that accepts credit cards. Because of the convenience provided, you should not be opposed to obtaining a debit card. There are two cautions when using the debit card.

- If you fail to record and monitor the use of your debit card, you can overdraft your checking account. The result is charges and fees.

- If your debit card is tied in to a credit card, failure to monitor your account can result in charges on your credit card.

The debit card is an extension of your checking account and should be treated as such; record each transaction in your check book. This will insure that you do not lose control of your spending.

NOTES TO SELF

_____

_____

LOANS TO CHILDREN

As you plan your retirement, your goal is to save money through investments, annuities, and qualified retirement funds (IRA, etc.). As these funds build and as you reach retirement, or are close thereto, the children will notice you have a little excess money. It is at this point that your children and maybe other relatives or associates will come up with 101 of the most ingenious, worthwhile, unique reasons why you should loan them your money so they can meet their goals. Usually these loans are made with no interest charged, no promissory note signed, and no payments arranged for or made. When you hit retirement, you cannot count on these funds to help you through the "golden years."

I believe you should absolutely not, definitely not, and under no conditions, make loans of retirement funds to your children. In almost every instance when you make a loan to one of your children, it is never paid back. A loan to children, for some reason, is usually considered a gift, and they have no intention or desire to repay it. Loans to other relatives and associates fall into a close second in the rankings of loans never repaid. In many instances the quality of your retirement depends on these funds. When they are not repaid, the quality of your life style and medical attention suffers.

For those who have already fallen into this trap, let me offer several suggestions that will hopefully help you recover:

- Insist that the individual make monthly payments to repay the loan.
- Keep a complete and accurate accounting of all payments made and balances due.
- Require interest payments on all outstanding balances.
- Put the loan on a promissory note signed and kept in your possession. (A copy of a standard promissory note appears at the end of this chapter.)
- Let all of your children know about loans to other children.
- If the child does not repay the loan on time, break his legs or twist his neck, or do whatever will cause him or her to be responsible. Your retirement is at stake.
- If the loan is not repaid, reduce that child's inheritance, if any, by the amount of the outstanding balance of the loan.
- On loans to other individuals, turn the promissory note over to an attorney for collection if they default on repayment.

If you do not have the ability to say *no* to your children, place your funds in a hard-to-get to investment. Annuities and Long Term CD's may have a penalty for early withdrawal, which makes it easier to say *no*.

NOTES TO SELF

_____

_____

_____

BUYING VEHICLES

When I was a kid, I remember on several occasions my mother and father getting up on a Saturday morning and saying, "Let's go look at cars." I remember on those occasions that by noon they always came home with a brand-new car. There is nothing like the smell of a new car. To some people, a car is a tool to be used for transportation to achieve other purposes. To some it is a status symbol—the fancier the car, or the bigger the truck, the more important I am. Some people take weeks to buy a car; others, like my parents, buy on impulse. In our society, a car or truck is essential. Transportation unlocks the keys to all of the necessities and pleasures of life. Having experienced many of these feelings, I now give my opinion on how to purchase and use cars and trucks.

In my younger days, one could buy a new car for $2,000. Inflation has changed that, and now a new car ranges from $15,000 to $40.000. I purchased my first home with 3 ½ acres for $29,000. Now half the cars on the market cost more than I paid for my original home. Because of the extreme costs of buying a new car, I believe you should never buy one in less than a week. Shop around, take your time, look for a good deal, and if after a week you still decide you *need* it, you will then be in a position to make an educated decision on the purchase.

When I purchased my first new car, I drove it around the block and lost one-third of the value, because then it was a used car. I have since found that I can purchase a used vehicle for a substantial amount less than the original cost and let someone else lose the depreciation. If you take time to shop around, you can purchase a used car that looks like new, smells like new, has low mileage, and may still have an original factory warranty on it. The savings in purchasing a car of this type is substantial, and you can now place those saved funds into an investment toward retirement.

I know some people who, every two or three years, trade in their vehicle for a new one. For good reasons, I don't believe this should be done. Those who follow this practice are making a car payment every month for their entire lives. If you buy a car and take good care of it, it should last for 250,000 miles. When it is paid for, you will save from $300 to $500 per month on payments you don't have to make. That money, when invested regularly towards retirement, will be a substantial sum and may make a huge difference in the life style you live after retirement. When the costs of repairs exceed the market value of the vehicle, it is time to get rid of it. There are always people out there who are willing to pay cash for a well used vehicle. I believe you should drive the vehicle until it wears out; then if no one buys it, haul it to the junk yard and get a new used vehicle.

When you retire, it is extremely important that you have a good, reliable, low-mileage vehicle to see you through your retirement years. If you are fortunate enough to live another 45 years after retirement, which I hope you do, you may have to purchase another vehicle somewhere along the line. If you follow the above practices and start at a early age, you should have the cash to get your next used vehicle.

NOTES TO SELF

_____

_____

_____

CELL PHONES

When you retire, your kids, for some reason, suddenly believe you have become old, senile and incapacitated; they want you to check in every morning, every night, and whenever you leave the home. In fact, some of them even want you to get a cell phone so they can keep track of you at all times. A cell phone is a wonderful thing if you are not opposed to being found. However, if at times you want a little peace and quiet, cell phones can certainly be a detriment to your peace and quiet. On the other hand, a cell phone is better than standing in the rain at a phone booth.

Cell phones have a lot of ranges and plans. I've found you can get a good plan for about $40.00 per month that will enable you to communicate with the family from wherever you may be. Be cautious when you get a plan, because most companies will tie you in for a year with heavy penalties for early cancellation. If you travel a lot, you may want to get a plan that is good nationwide, with no roaming charges. Roaming charges are the fees you must pay when your phone calls are routed through a system that is not part of your cell phone's service. They become very expensive in some areas and should be avoided if at all possible.

One final note on cell phones: If your children want to keep track of you that closely, let them buy you the cell phone. It will save $40.00 per month, which you can spend on other things during retirement.

NOTES TO SELF

_____

_____

COMPUTERS

A computer is not a galactic spy system placed in your home, to monitor your every move, spy on your finances, report

29

your whereabouts, and explode and destroy the neighborhood if you hit the wrong button. Many retired people are scared to death of computers and absolutely refuse to get one, use one, or learn about one. I had an aunt who felt the same way about automobiles. She never learned to drive, and she seldom traveled. In her mature years she was held captive by her inability to move around. You too may be held captive by your inability to use the computer. Almost everything in our society is operated or controlled by computers. Your car runs on computers, your credit card is run on computers, your investments and bank accounts are controlled through computers, and when you buy groceries at a grocery store you are checked out through computers. Computers are such a totally integrated part of our life, you need to become familiar with computers and use them for your benefit.

Your computer can be connected to the Internet through your telephone line, a DSL line, or a transmitter. Each of these methods will give you instant access to all of your accounts 24 hours a day. I prefer my DSL because I don't have the patience to wait for the dial-up service. The DSL is very fast, but the type of service you are able to access will depend on what type of service is available in your local area. It is extremely important that you be connected to the Internet. Without this connection, your computer will be limited to word processing and bookkeeping-type skills. The Internet is your door to the world, because so many things are available on the Internet. Note: many things on the Internet are not good. You must control your access to web sites and limit them to those things which are good, uplifting and beneficial.

All your finances and investments can be controlled, tracked or changed by using the computer. When I travel, I buy my airline tickets through my computer-Internet connection. I can rent a car, book hotel rooms, and schedule cruises—all on the computer. In fact, I can buy almost anything on my computer while sitting in my office or at home. I check the news, the weather, and stock quotes and watch movies on my computer. In fact, I can also write letters, send emails, distribute pictures, and tie into government agency records through my computer. I recommend you get and use a computer.

There are several types of computers you can purchase. Some people use what is called a laptop, which is not much bigger than two books. I have a laptop. I also have a desk computer. If you prefer a stationary computer, the desk computer will work for you. When you obtain a computer, go to a good computer store, where plenty of professionals can help pick one that is just right for you. You should be able to get a complete computer system with a color printer for somewhere between $1,200 to $1,500. Shop around. Do not get the first one you see.

NOTES TO SELF

_____

_____

PROMISSORY NOTE

$_____

Date _____

AS HEREINAFTER AGREED, for value received, I/we, jointly and severally, promise to pay to the order of (Name)_____ _____ at (City)_____, (State)__ _____, with interest at the rate of _____ per cent per annum from this date until paid. It is hereby agreed that the said $_____ dollars shall be paid in installments of not less than $_____ dollars per month, together with interest upon the balance remaining unpaid beginning (month)_____ __, (year)_____, and on or before the (date)_____ day of every

31

month thereafter until the whole amount of the principal and interest is paid. Should default be made in the payment of any installment at the time when the same is above promised to be paid, then the whole unpaid amount shall become immediately due and payable. In the event default is made in any of the above payments and said note is placed in the hands of an attorney for collection or suit is brought on the same, an additional amount of _____ per cent of the amount found due shall be added to the same as collection fees.

_____

Husband (person borrowing)

_____

Wife (person borrowing)

CHAPTER THREE

INVESTING

GET IN THE RACE

The summer of my fourteenth birthday, I started working full-time in a grocery store. I worked 40 to 50 hours a week, attended high school, graduated and went to college. During that six-year period I earned a lot of money, for a boy, and I spent it all. I had no concept of investments, nor had I ever heard of the stock market, mutual funds, CDs, annuities, rentals or other business opportunities. In other words, I didn't know a thing about savings or preparing for the future. Now as I look back on that time period, had I taken a small portion of the money I wasted, put it into investments and left it alone, I would have had a substantial amount of money at the present time. A $100 investment per month at 6% interest, over that six-year period, would have given me over $130,000 at the present time.

There are many types of investments. I will not cover them all, only several of the major investments used today. It is imperative that you get in the race; start investing *now*!

STOCKS

We hear a great deal about the stock market. Stock markets are exchanges where ownership interests in businesses are bought and sold. These interests in the ownership of a business are in the form of stocks, that is, a stock certificate for X amount of shares of stock. For example, were you to buy 100 shares of stock in General Motors Corporation®, at $10 a share, a $1,000 investment, you would receive a stock certificate which shows you own 100 shares of the corporation. What does this mean to you? It means you have a right to a share of the profits and dividends of the corporation. If the corporation does well and the value of the stock goes up, you can sell the stock and make a profit. If you sell the stock for $20 a share, that is, $2,000, you will make a profit of $1,000. This is how money may be made when you invest in the stock market.

Many thousands of corporations sell their stocks in the stock markets to raise capital to run their corporations. When a corporation does well, the value of the stock goes up; and when a corporation does poorly, the value of the stock goes down. When you invest in the stock market, you must be prepared for the fluctuating values of the investment. Many people have made a great deal of money in the market. At the same time, many people have lost a great deal of money in the market.

In order to buy stock you must use an investment broker who is licensed to buy and sell stocks. There is a fee charged for such services; that is how the broker earns a living. Because of the volatility of the stock market, it is imperative that you have a broker who works for a reputable brokerage firm and is someone you can trust with your money. Because of the high risk of investing in this market, you must not invest money you cannot afford to lose. Be cautious when investing; however, if you have a broker who is well trained and trustworthy, you can make substantial profits over a period of time.

It is important to note that the younger you start investing in this market, the better results you will have when you reach retirement. I wish I had invested in the stock market while I was still a teenager. Now that I am more mature, I must be more conservative in my investments and not take as many risks as I could have when I was younger.

NOTES TO SELF

_____

_____

MUTUAL FUNDS

It is difficult to be able to pick a winning stock. The principles of economics that make corporations successful and drive the stock markets are so complex that unless an individual is involved in it full-time, he or she is unable to make a proper investment decision. Even individuals who are full time in the business cannot always pick a winner. In order to spread the risk inherent in the stock market, many investors have turned to *Mutual Funds* as a way to invest and control the risk of loss.

A mutual fund is created when a number of people invest their money into a pool that is managed by a professional. The manager, using the money from the investors, purchases stocks in many corporations. When purchasing mutual funds, you do not actually purchase stock in the stock market; you purchase an interest in the pool that owns stock in many corporations. The advantage to buying mutual funds over a regular stock investment is that your risk of investment loss is spread. If one of the corporations owned by the pool goes bankrupt, the other corporations are still good, and you don't lose all your investment.

There are thousands of mutual funds to choose from. You can purchase these investments from your regular stock broker, from some insurance companies, or from investment advisors. Many IRA's and 401(k) plans use mutual funds as the underlying investment of their funds. The use of mutual funds for retirement investing is a huge industry, and I encourage you to look at this market.

Remember, in order to protect your investment, you must use a reputable company and a professional you can trust.

NOTES TO SELF

_____

_____

REAL ESTATE

Real Estate (property) is one of the great investments in our country. Billions of dollars are invested in real estate, and billions of dollars are made on the return of these investments. I believe real estate has been and still is a great investment for retirement. Let me impress upon you a few pointers that may help in this process.

- Because most investment of real estate requires a substantial amount of money, you should begin investing at a young age. This is particularly important because most mortgages run from 15 to 30 years. The more years you invest before retirement, the more likely these investments will be free and clear by the time you reach retirement age.

- Your investment in real estate should produce a cash flow sufficient to make the payments on the investment. If you have a negative cash flow, you will have to draw money from another source to make the payments.

- If you invest in an area going through a deteriorating stage, it will probably have less value in the future than when you bought it. It will also be less marketable, and you may find it difficult to get the money out when you need it for retirement.

- Many people believe that owning a home is a liability because it does not produce income. However, I believe that by the time you reach retirement, you must own a home, and it must be free and clear of debt. Yes, there are problems with medical care and aid, but if your home is free and clear, you can't be thrown out as long as you pay your taxes. If you rent, you still have to pay all the utilities, insurance, and taxes even if you pay them to someone other than the government. The landlord is paying these expenses and you are paying him or her to pay them.

- When dealing with real estate, you must have a good professional real estate advisor—one who knows the market, is reliable, and will be there to work with you when you sell your investment.

These views are mine. There are those who believe totally opposite. You must make the best investment to fit your situation. Your challenge, if you intend to invest in real estate, is to find someone reputable who can aid you in making a successful real estate investment. Remember, there are thousands of people who bought investment lots in Arizona, New Mexico and Texas for $5,000 or $10,000 and gave them away to charity or walked away from them because they were worth only $300 to $500. On the other hand, there are many who start making investments at a young age and retire with a large estate and a good, solid annual return on their investments. When investing in real estate, the latter should be your goal, and it can be achieved if you follow sound principles and work with good advisors.

NOTES TO SELF

_____

_____

_____

OWNING YOUR OWN BUSINESS

There are many ways to invest, but in the minds of many people, the idea of investing has been to give your money to someone else, like a bank, let them manage the assets, and in the process you earn a profit while you work as an employee for someone else. The fact of the matter is that very few people become wealthy or accumulate a large estate just working for someone else. I have always recommended that where possible, you own your own business. Every successful business, whether it be General Motors®, General Electric®, or Kinkos®, is the result of someone starting their own business. It is not always necessary to quit your current job in order to start your own business. However, it is necessary that you have the guts (intestinal fortitude) to do more than just work your eight-hour job.

In order to have your own business, several components are essential:

- You must have capital (money) to get started and maintain the business until it turns a profit. Not having enough money when you start is one of the biggest causes of business failure.

- You must have a product or service that is needed or wanted in society (such as Kinkos® copies or Subway® sandwiches).

- You must have a marketing system that delivers your product or service. The best product or service in the world is worthless if you cannot get it to customers.

- You must have competent, professional advisors to help you establish your business. The minimum professionals you need are:

    i.   A bank or credit union to assist with your financing or money management.
    ii. A CPA to assist with your books, records and taxes.
    iii. An insurance man for liability protection.
    iv. A marketing expert to get your product to the customer.
    v.   An attorney to make sure you meet all the legal requirements.

There are risks in starting your own business; a very high percentage of them fail within the first two or three years. In order to succeed, you must give yourself the very best shot by using your professionals and by having a service or product that is marketable. You could start a million different types of businesses and the rewards for success are great. If you are faint-hearted or do not have the ability to follow through, a business of your own may not be for you.

My final word on a business of your own is what I always tell my clients: "If you are going duck hunting, you must go where the ducks are." Translation: A supermarket in Orwell, Vermont is probably not a good idea.

NOTES TO SELF

_____

_____

MANAGING YOUR OWN BUSINESS

When choosing the type of business entity under which you will be doing business, you must consult with your CPA. There are a number of choices: Sole Proprietorships, General Partnerships, Limited Partnerships, Limited Liability Companies, Sub Chapter S Corporations, and C Corporations. The type of business entity you choose will depend on what you want to accomplish, and only your CPA can give you the tax ramifications of each.

Over the past 30 years, I have found that many business entities do not function properly as a business. The liabilities are huge. I offer the following recommendations to help you avoid the pitfalls of improper business practices.

41

- Make sure you file proper documentation with state agencies.
    i. Articles of Incorporation
    ii. Articles of Organization
    iii. Annual Reports

- Always hold required business meetings.
    i. Management meetings
    ii. Board of directors meetings
    iii. Shareholders meetings

- Always keep proper minutes of meetings
    Failure to keep required minutes of all meetings is the biggest error made by small businesses. When a lawsuit is brought against a business, the lack of business minutes will expose all of your personal assets to business liability (your home, car, checking & savings, etc.).

- Keep proper financial records
    i. Balance sheets
    ii. Profit & Loss statements
    iii. Net worth

- Always file your tax returns on time.

- Give regular reports to partners, members or shareholders.
    Failure to keep all interested parties notified of "what is going on" results in hard feelings, breakups and law suits.

NOTES TO SELF

_____

_____

QUALIFIED PLANS

Retired people worry about three things more than anything else. Although these three are not the only things to worry about, they seem to occupy most of the worry time. The first is family. They worry about how the family will make it—financially, educationally, healthwise, employment, spouse problems, children, grandchildren, where they live, will they come to visit, will they stay too long, won't they come to visit, and so on. I discuss the topic of family in more depth later. The second cause of worry is health. This problem is huge to those who are fortunate enough to mature in years. A few are lucky enough to escape health problems, but the rest must cope with declining physical abilities and associated health problems. This, too, I cover in another section. The third item of great concern is money. I have never met a person who thought he or she had too much money, but I have met many who worry that they do not. This section is about money for retirement.

My father worked for the local city water department. He started as a laborer in the early 40's and worked his way up the employment line until he became the assistant superintendent of the water department. One year the city administration changed, and he was demoted to the trenches. His wages were cut, and the ensuing stress eventually caused him to suffer a heart attack. He ended up with a medical retirement at the age of 58. Within one year my mother died from cancer. From that time until my father's death, he worried about money. Because he had lived through the depression of the 1930's, money was a big issue to him. He did anything he could to conserve what little he had, things such as not turning on the lights when it became dark, or the fan to get cool. In the winter he would not open the drapes or curtains to let light in because the heat would escape though the windows. He wouldn't go anywhere because it cost for the gas. The story goes on and on, but the gist of it is that it did not matter what time of day I went to see him, he would be sitting in front of the fireplace, in the dark, worrying about money. He didn't think he had enough money. This problem consumed every waking hour and probably most of his sleeping hours.

There are many ways to accumulate money for retirement. It's not that we lack methods, it's that most of us don't start early enough. We don't put enough away, and we don't leave it alone long enough for it to grow.

There are some things we can and must do to accumulate money for retirement. The first is to get into some type of a qualified retirement program. That is to say, get into a 401(k), 403(b), simple IRA, SEP-IRA, or some other type of retirement account. You can put away money untaxed and let it grow for retirement. *This is a must for retirement.* There are a few, but very few, who don't need this planning, but my name is not Rockefeller, and yours probably isn't either. So just get on with it, do it, or suffer the consequences later.

A qualified retirement plan allows you to put money into a savings or investment plan for retirement. The amount you place in the qualified plan is allowed as a deduction from your taxable income on your 1040 Tax Return in the year it is placed in the account. Since this is a retirement account, the money is intended to stay there until you retire. If you take the money out before the age of 59½ , it will be taxed in the year of withdrawal, and you will also pay a 10% penalty. In other words, *do not take the money out until retirement.*

In many situations, *you* will have to put all the money into the account. However, those of you who are more fortunate may be employed by an employer who will match funds which you place in the retirement account. This is a blessing, or good luck, or whatever you want to call it, because the amount your employer puts in the account is free money to you. Anyone who has the opportunity to receive these matching funds and does not is one brick short of a load. That is to say, they missed the boat. How about stupid?

44

The amount you are allowed to place in a retirement account varies, depending on the plan available. The minimum you place in your account will depend on how much you can afford to put away. The maximum will depend on the type of plan you qualify for. There are higher limits for more complex types of plans, usually for those who are self-employed or own their own business. The bottom line is to put away as much as you can. In this area, you must force yourself. If we are left to our own vices, we tend to spend what we have and a little more. Thus we have little or none to put away. You must discipline yourself to put away as much as possible, even to the point it hurts, as often as possible for as long as possible.

This book is not a definitive explanation of retirement plans. What you must know is that you should be involved in a plan, and there are many qualified professionals out there who can help you. Your bank, your insurance representative, your broker, your benefits office and your financial advisor should all be able to give you direction on these accounts.

The following is a list of some types of Qualified plans:[1]

- Simple IRA
- Traditional IRA
- Roth IRA
- 401(k)
- 403(b)
- 457
- Defined Contribution Plan
- Defined Benefit Plan

I do want to mention one additional item on the subject of IRA's. I believe the very best thing the average working person can do is fund a ROTH IRA, an IRA funded by after-tax money. As opposed to all the other types of qualified retirement plans that have been mentioned, which are funded by before tax money, the ROTH gives you no tax benefits on your 1040 return when you place money in the account. However, the ROTH pays big dividends (figuratively speaking) when the money is taken out after retirement. The Growth in the ROTH account comes out untaxed. That is to say, you do not pay taxes on the gain. So when you retire and take your money out of the ROTH, it is all yours to keep and spend as you want.[2]

NOTES TO SELF

_____

_____

_____

ANNUITIES

The term *annuity* confuses many people. The reason is that you hear it in so many different settings. Many companies, when you retire, give you an annuity, and insurance companies invest your money in annuities. An annuity is simply a vehicle used to accumulate money for investment purposes or retirement. Annuities can either be qualified, such as an IRA, or non-qualified with no pre-tax dollars in the investment.

Many companies that have a retirement program accumulate or credit their employees with funds towards retirement. When people retire, they generally have several options.[3]

- They can take their retirement money in a lump sum, which is generally invested by the retiree to provide for future needs.
- The company will pay retirees a certain amount of money for the rest of their lives.
- The company buys an annuity that makes payment to retirees for the rest of their lives.

An annuity of this type guarantees payment of a certain amount of money to the annuitant (retired person) for a certain period of time or until death. At present many retired people in the country receive retirement payments in the form of an annuity. Several items are critically important when a person retires:

- Many companies give their retirees the opportunity to take their retirement annuity for only the retiree. In this instance, a surviving spouse receives nothing.

- When you split a retirement annuity between you and your spouse, the benefits received are reduced 25% to 35%.

- Many people take the retirement annuity for themselves, not including the spouse, because they get more money. A portion of the extra money is then invested in life insurance to protect the surviving spouse.

It is imperative as you reach retirement that you meet with your legal and financial advisors to determine which options are best for you. The wrong decision can result in terrible consequences. Harold retired with all the retirement in his name because his wife was in ill health and he knew she would pass away before he did. This decision was based on a physical examination by Harold's physician who told Harold he was in good health. One week after Harold retired, he died of a heart attack. His wife, who received not a single penny from his retirement, lived another 18 years. Do not make such a decision without competent, professional help.

You can purchase annuities from almost any insurance company. This purchase can be done either by depositing a lump sum or in monthly payments. Each company has an option as to what type of investment your annuity funds go into. You can place the investment into a fixed account that pays a fixed amount of interest; it is not invested in stocks or mutual funds. You can place the investment into mutual funds or stocks, in which case the return on the annuity will depend on the return of the investment. If the stock market goes up, you make money; if it goes down, you lose money.

You may take your money out of the annuity by several methods:

- You can take it all out in a single lump sum.
- You can take it out in varying amounts at will.
- You can take it out in annuity payments—X amount of dollars for a specific period of time or until death
- You can take it in payments for your life or for the life of you and your spouse jointly.

There are many options to consider. You must understand that you need professional assistance in order to select the type of annuity and the payment option best for you. You must note that once a contract is signed for an annuity or a payment option, it *cannot be changed*. If you make the wrong selection, you are stuck with it. Get competent help to make these decisions.

Annuities are an excellent investment vehicle. I recommend that you include at least one in your investment portfolio.

NOTES TO SELF

_____

_____

_____

BANK OR CREDIT UNION SAVINGS

In this section I will treat both banks and credit unions the same. This will give heartburn to many bankers because banks feel they are superior to credit unions. However, the investments in both of these types of financial institutions are so similar that what applies to one also applies to the other. Large amounts of money are placed in retirement accounts in both institutions. These accounts are relatively safe and can provide some security in retirement. Most banks are federally insured under the FDIC (Federal Deposit Insurance Corporation). Most credit unions are insured under the NCUA (National Credit Union Administration). Both institutions give security for savings in the retirement years. Both banks and credit unions have several types of accounts to choose from:

- Checking accounts allow you to write checks at will. These accounts can also be accessed with debit cards. Many checking accounts do not pay interest on the amounts in the account. If you have an account that does not pay interest, change the account to one that does. If your financial institution does not have an account that pays interest, change to one that does. Do not be afraid to change financial institutions. Remember, you are the one paying for the service, so if you don't get the service you want, change to an institution that will give the desired service. Do not keep large amounts of money in these accounts. I believe you should keep in a checking account the amount of money you will use over a two-to three-month period; any excess over that amount should be in an account that pays more interest.

- Regular savings accounts, in the past referred to as "passbook savings," are used by many people. These accounts are easy to add funds to and easy to withdraw from. The interest in these accounts is usually very low, and may be below 1%. It is not a good idea to keep large amounts of money in these accounts because the interest rate is so low. If you have an account of this type, the amount of money in it should be limited to the cash needed over a three- to six-month period. I call this the emergency fund, because it is easy to get to in case of an emergency.

- Many financial institutions have what is referred to as Money Market accounts, the next step up in the investment order. These accounts pay higher interest than do regular savings, but not much higher. They are easy to access and usually do not impose a penalty when funds are withdrawn from them. I do not believe you should have both a regular savings account and a money market account. Choose one or the other and put the rest in CDs.

- Certificates of Deposit are usually referred to as CDs. These funds are placed in the investment for periods of time generally ranging from three months to five years. The interest rate will vary depending on the length of time the investment runs. The longer the time periods for a CD, the higher the interest rate. The CD almost always pays a higher interest rate than do money market funds. The CD is the favored investment for money placed in the bank. However, you need to know that any early withdrawal of funds from the CD will result in a penalty. Thus you will not want to place your funds in a CD for a longer period than when you will need the money. The penalty for early withdrawal is usually the amount of interest you would earn in a 90-day period. For three-month CDs, the penalty is usually the interest you would earn in one month.

Most banks and credit unions are relatively safe. Strict rules and regulations are placed on these financial institutions to ensure proper use of invested money. With these regulations in place, very few financial institutions of this type fail. Yet some perform better than others. With this in mind, may I suggest several things when choosing a financial institution:

- Larger banks and credit unions usually have better trained professional employees than do small ones.
- Check the credit rating of your financial institution.
- Is it friendly and courteous? Some are not.

- Single-branch banks and credit unions may not be managed in an efficient manner, or pay a competitive interest rate.
- Does it have credit and debit cards?
- Is it insured under FDIC or NCUA?
- Are current customers satisfied with the service they receive?
- Does it have overdraft protection without charging you an arm and leg?
- What are the fees charged? Many institutions charge large fees and charge for every service.
- Does it have a large turnover in employees so that every time you go in the faces have changed?
- Ask why? Get an answer.
- Compare interest rates. Many times a credit union will pay higher interest than a bank.

NOTES TO SELF

_____

_____

_____

REVERSE MORTGAGES

I do not believe one's home should be considered an investment, though it is an asset that must be considered. I have always believed that one's home should be free and clear and in one's own name, or in the name of a Trust, at the time of retirement. This guarantees that you will always have a place to live in your retirement years. However, many who retire do not have the financial means to maintain their lifestyle or meet their needs in retirement. In the past few years, the Reverse Mortgage has become a tool that allows you to live in your home and at the same time use the equity in your home to supplement the costs of retirement, whatever they may be.[4]

A Reverse Mortgage works like this. You obtain a loan based on the equity in your home, called a Reverse Mortgage, and the lender makes payments to you. You never make payments to the lender. You can receive payments in whatever manner you determine, that is, lump sum, regular payments, as a line of credit or a combination of these options. In this manner you can access the funds as needed, and there are no restrictions on what you use the money for. Many people use it for medical expenses, life insurance or long-term care insurance, or to supplement an insufficient income. You are permitted to live in the home as long as you live. Upon your demise, the home is generally sold to pay the mortgage; and excess amounts after the mortgage is paid, if any, can be paid to your family or your estate.[5]

When you obtain a Reverse Mortgage, there is no liability to you and your spouse other than the equity you have in the home, nor is there any liability to your children or your heirs. In those instances when the amounts owed on the Reverse Mortgage are in excess of the value of the home, when it is sold, there is no liability to you or the family members. In other words, the family does not have to pay the difference to the mortgage company. For example, if you die and the property sells for $150,000, but the mortgage company is owed $200,000, you do not have to pay the $50,000 extra to the mortgage company.

The cost to set up a Reverse Mortgage can be very high. This process makes the funds available to you. You generally do not have to pay the setup fees; however, the costs for the setup generally become a lien on your property and will eventually have to be paid even if you do not take or use any money.

Over the past few years I have watched with interest what people do with the proceeds from a Reverse Mortgage. Although I believe the Reverse Mortgage a very good retirement tool, I am concerned that many people fritter away the proceeds carelessly. One couple used the proceeds to take a trip to New England to see the trees in the fall, without giving thought to potential medical needs not covered. I recommend, therefore, that if you get a Reverse Mortgage, you be very cautious in how you use the money.

A Reverse Mortgage requires mandatory counseling by the US Department of Housing and Urban Development. I also recommend that you meet with your own financial counselors and attorney.

NOTES TO SELF

_____

_____

_____

INFLATION

As a teenager, working in the grocery store in the 1950s, I observed the price of food products: bananas, ten cents a pound; grapes, ten cents a pound; bread, four loaves for a dollar; milk, fifty cents a gallon; a good steak, $.39 a pound. In 1971, I bought a home with 3½ acres for $29,000. It's now worth $400,000. I bought a new suburban for $6,000. The cost of a new suburban now is more than I can count. This phenomenon of the eternal increase in prices is called *inflation*. It has always been with us and will always be with us.

A challenge we have is that after we retire, the prices continue to go up, but our income is fixed and does not keep up with the rise of prices. This challenge has increased recently because we now live longer. Someone who retires at age 65 and lives to age

95 has thirty years of living on a fixed income while the price of everything goes up. As you reach retirement, you must have some method to cope with inflation. A few helpful suggestions are as follows:

- Investments in real estate tend to increase with inflation.
- Regular bank or credit union savings normally do not keep up with inflation, but they are very safe.
- Some investments in equities are safer than others to help keep up with inflation.
- If you start early and have a large retirement fund, your investments should grow to keep up with inflation.
- If your daddy is rich or your children are rich, they can help you out.

If you fail to plan for inflation, as you move toward retirement, you may end up at the poverty level. Do something early, and do it often. This will give you some options when retirement comes.

NOTES TO SELF

_____

_____

_____

Note: A final word on investments is *diversify.* "Don't place all you eggs in one basket," a saying I always heard while growing up, is correct. Have a qualified plan, and also have some CDs. Own some real estate, have your own business, own some equities or mutual funds or both. A variety of investment tools will spread your risk and increase your chance of financial success. The quality of your retirement will depend on your success in investment.

CHAPTER FOUR

TAXES

DON'T CROSS THE IRS

The IRS is an official in this race of life, and you don't want the officials mad at you. If you follow the tax rules it is easier to get to the finish line. Failure to deal properly with taxes and know the tax law can result in fines, penalties or payment of excess taxes. Only a professional can help you maneuver through the tax maize. A good CPA will always put you ahead in the race.

INCOME TAXES

This is not a treatise on income tax, nor will I attempt to explain income taxes. I don't believe the IRS even has the ability to explain income taxes. However, you must keep in mind a few points on income tax, as you move toward retirement.

- Always file your tax returns on time!
- Do not fail to take your minimum distribution on qualified money and report it on your return.
- A good CPA who prepares your returns will protect you from audits.
- If audited, you get better results if you treat the IRS agent with respect. After all, he is a human being also.
- Always be honest in preparing your income tax returns—no regrets.
- Take *all* the legal deductions allowed by law.

57

People often say, "I don't want to make more money because it throws me into a higher tax bracket." My reply has always been the same, "Would you rather make $20,000 and pay no taxes, or would you rather make $100,000 and pay $20,000 taxes?" You do the math. Realize that taxes are a part of our society. It is our cost for being in the greatest country in the world. Travel abroad, look around, and you will find we've got a bargain.

NOTES TO SELF

_____

_____

TAXES ON QUALIFIED MONEY

All the money in qualified plans is untaxed. Qualified plans include IRAs, 401(k)s, and any other money that has never been taxed on your 1040 Return. The IRS is very jealous about its taxes and insists that these monies be taxed. The time for taxation will vary, depending on the circumstances of each individual account. Here are some guidelines, but you must rely on your CPA to give you directions. General rules are as follows:

- All money will be taxed.
- The tax must be paid in the year the money is withdrawn from the account.
- If money is withdrawn before age 59½, there is a 10% penalty.
- You must take distributions under the minimum distribution rules by age 70½. Failure to take these distributions results in a 50% penalty.
- If you pass away, your surviving spouse can put these accounts in his or her name.

- Your children can be made beneficiaries of these accounts (this can delay payment of taxes for many years).
- You can schedule withdrawals so a withdrawal does not throw you into a higher tax bracket.

Your CPA can give you counsel in all of these issues.

If, on your demise, a form 706 Federal Estate Tax Return is required, you will not only pay estate taxes on qualified money, you will still have to pay income taxes. There is no stepped-up basis on qualified money.

NOTES TO SELF

_____

_____

ESTATE TAXES

Over the years, governments have received a great deal of their financing through estate and inheritance taxes. These are taxes levied against a person's estate when that person dies. These taxes are usually levied on a graduated percentage of your total estate.[6] The result is that the larger your estate, the higher percentage you pay in taxes. Several states impose no inheritance tax, but most do. You can check either on the internet or with a professional in your state to find if there is a tax and what the rates are. The Federal Estate Tax applies to everyone. The chart below shows the current status of the Federal Estate Tax rates.

ESTATE TAX CREDIT AND EXEMPTIONS

Year	Unified Credit	Exemption Equivalent
2005	$555,888	$1,500,000
2006-8	$780,800	$2,000,000
2009	$1,455,800	$3,500,000
2010	$0	$0
2011	$345,800	$1,000,000

If you find that your estate has a potential for taxation under the above chart, it is imperative that you contact and work with your CPA and attorney in developing an estate plan. It will save you taxes. Legal methods designed by Congress are in the Internal Revenue Code; they permit many exemptions or savings in the estate taxes. Such things as Martial Deduction Trusts, QTIP Trusts, ILIT Trusts, gifts to family and charity produce great savings when properly put in place. You must have professional help in these areas. Failure to use these tools in your estate planning can cost thousands and hundreds of thousands of dollars in estate taxes.

The Federal Estate Tax applies to everything you own at death. You will be taxed on your home, rentals, stocks and investments, retirement benefits, annuities, life insurance and personal property. Not even IRAs, 401(k)s or any qualified money is exempt from this tax. Note that even though you pay the estate tax on qualified money, you will still have to pay the income tax on these funds when they are taken out of the qualified plan. Because the rules regarding qualified plans are complicated, you must work with a good CPA to avoid the pitfalls of withdrawing these funds; the penalties for improper withdrawal are huge.

Just as the penalty for improper withdrawal from qualified plans is huge, so are the tax consequences for failure to do proper estate planning. For example, under the Federal Estate Tax Law for the year 2006, a $4,000,000 estate properly planned will pay no

Federal Estate Taxes, assuming there is a surviving spouse. However, if you fail to properly do your estate planning, the potential estate tax liability could be as much as $780,800—a terrible price to pay for failure to do proper planning. Do yourself a favor—go see your attorney and CPA.

NOTES TO SELF

_____

_____

_____

GIFT TAXES

You may believe that if you give your assets away while you are alive, they will not be taxed. Wrong! Just as there is a tax on all assets you own at your death, there is also a tax on gifts you give during your lifetime. There are no restrictions as to whom you may give gifts to, such as governments, schools, churches, charities, and other individuals. However, there are exemptions on gifts you give. These exemptions vary depending on the nature of the recipient of the gift.[7] The Federal Gift Tax rate is not the same rate as the Federal Estate Tax rate (see CHART #1 below), and both taxes use a different Unified Credit to determine taxability. (See CHART #2 below.) Compare this chart with the Estate Tax Credit and Exemptions Chart above. If you give a gift and use your Unified Credit on your gift tax return, that amount will also be deducted on your Federal Estate Tax return. If this is very confusing to you, talk to your CPA.

CHART #1
TOP TAX BRACKETS

Year	Estate	Gift
2005	47.00%	47.00%
2006	46.00%	46.00%
2007-9	45.00%	45.00%
2010	0.00%	35.00%
2011	55.00%	55.00%

CHART #2
GIFT TAX CREDIT AND EXEMPTIONS

Year	Unified Credit	Exemption Equivalent
2002-9	$345,800	$1,000,000
2010	$330,800	$1,000,000
2011	$345,800	$1,000,000

The practical aspect of the Federal Gift Tax is that it allows you to share some of your wealth with family and charities. For example, in the year 2006 you could have given $11,000 to every individual you desire with no gift tax consequence. If you have ten grandchildren, you could have given each of them $11,000 and your spouse could have given an equal amount; thus you could have given $220,000 to your grandchildren tax free. The amount of the annual exemption will be adjusted up annually by the IRS. Using these gifts, you can benefit your family and at the same time reduce the size of your estate. If you give gifts larger than the annual exclusion, the excess will apply to your Federal Unified Credit.

If you desire to benefit a charity of your choice, you can give gifts and receive an exemption for those gifts, and thus pay no tax on the transfer. These gifts can take the form of an outright gift or a future gift in the form of a CRUT (Charitable Remainder Uni

Trust) or CRAT (Charitable Remainder Annuity Trust). You can also make the charity the beneficiary of a life insurance policy. In many of these gifts to charity you may also receive a charitable gift deduction on your 1040 Income Tax Return. If the gift is made at your death, you can receive a charitable deduction on your Federal Estate Tax Return.

All this is very complicated, but your attorney and CPA understand the details and can give you direction. I would like to emphasize one extremely important thing: when you make a gift to family members, do not give money you will need to support yourself in retirement, either for living or medical expenses. I have found that when you give a gift to a child, if you need the money back, it is gone. You cannot get it back. Likewise, when you make a gift to a charity, you must in fact want to make a charitable gift. It is imperative that you understand what you will receive and what will go to the charity. Once you have entered into these contracts for gifts to charity, you can not change them or back out.

NOTES TO SELF

_____

_____

NOTE! CHANGES IN ESTATE AND GIFT TAX LAWS.

The Federal Estate and Gift Tax law as stated in the previous two sections of this book is correct as we go to press. However, you need to know that big changes are in the making, maybe.

In July 2006 the U.S. House of Represenatives passed a new Estate and Gift Tax law. The U.S. Senate attempted to pass a similar new Estate and Gift Tax law in August 2006, but it failed to get the needed 60 votes by 4 votes.

The Estate and Gift Tax changes are a big political battlefield between the two major political parties that hold power in the House and Senate. Both parties are attempting to use the passage or non-passasge of this law as a means of embarrassing the other party and thus gain votes in the November 2006 election.

What you need to know is that the Estate and Gift Tax laws will change. When and how we do not know, but your attorney or CPA can keep you informed of the changes when they come, and make appropiate changes in your financial/estate/retirement plans as needed. Changes will come!

PROPERTY TAXES

Property taxes are assessed by the counties in which the property lies, and the amount of property taxes varies widely throughout the nation. In some areas the property tax payment may be as much as a mortgage payment. When you purchase property, the taxes are levied on the basis of the fair market value of the property. The amount you pay depends on the amount and number of assessments levied by the county. When you retire and your income becomes fixed,—that means it doesn't increase,—the property tax burden can become very heavy. Many times retired people tend to let their property taxes go for a year or two unpaid. Do not fall into this trap. Never let your property taxes go delinquent in the hopes that you will have more money in the future. Many individuals have literally lost their property to a tax sale because they were unable to make up delinquent taxes.

Some counties have senior citizen tax breaks on property taxes. Qualification for these discounted property taxes may depend on several factors, such as age, income, disability, etc. One of my clients received a 90% discount on his property taxes. Check with your local treasurer or assessor's office to see if you qualify for a tax break after retirement.

NOTES TO SELF

_____

_____

CHAPTER FIVE

INSURANCE

WHEN IT BENEFITS YOU

There are many types of insurance in the marketplace, and just as many insurance salesmen to sell them to you. I don't intend to discuss all the types, nor do I intend to recommend any particular insurance. Your needs will be different from most other people's, and therefore you will need to deal with your own insurance specialist. Your insurance specialist can point you to the best type of policy based on what you are trying to accomplish. I will explain some of the basic types of insurance and indicate some of the uses for each type. The proper use of insurance adds points to your race.

TERM LIFE INSURANCE

Term life insurance is insurance you purchase for a specific length of time; hence the time period is known as the *term*. These policies generally range from a period of one year to thirty years. The time usually is for a period of 1, 5, 10, 15, 20 or 30 years. However, they may be for any number of years.

The term policy is the least expensive of all types of life insurance. This is because you are only buying insurance. That is to say, there are no investment features in the policy, and there is generally no cash value in the policy. When you reach the end of the term period, the policy ends, and you have no insurance. Likewise, if you stop making the premium payments, the policy will end.

One of the best uses for the term policy is for young people who are just starting out. For example, a young couple who are married, have one child and are just out of school usually have a negative net worth, because they have student loans, a new car, and a new home. All their assets, if liquidated, could not pay all the debts. In this instance, term insurance can create an immediate estate. You can obtain a term policy for the amount of the debts, plus what it would take for a surviving spouse to put lives back in order. This provides that the spouse and child will not be forced out of the home and will be able to maintain their standard of living. It takes a substantial amount of money for a surviving spouse to recover. I generally recommend a policy that exceeds the debt by a minimum of $250,000. This amount will vary with each set of circumstances. For example, if the couple have four or five children, it will take more to rebuild the family than it will a couple with only one child.

Term insurance can also be used for such needs as business debt, buy-sell agreements, or a lack of money to purchase other types of insurance. It can be used to supplement permanent insurance when the need for insurance will decrease over a period of time, such as when a mortgage is paid off, or the amount your investments has grown. The cost of term insurance is a function of your age and your health. The older you are and the worse your health, the higher the cost of the insurance. However, if you purchase a level term policy, the premium will stay the same over the term of the policy. But if you get a renewable term policy, the premium will go up each time you extend or renew the policy.

WHOLE LIFE POLICIES

A whole life insurance policy is intended to be permanent. That is, it will remain in force during the entire life of the insured. The cash value of the whole life policies generally builds faster than it does for other types of policies; therefore, if you have a lot of extra cash, you may want to put it into this type of policy. The premiums are generally higher than those of the universal life policy, but over a long period of time the cash value will build to a substantial amount.

Many insurance salesmen believe this is the only type of policy to sell. If your agent wants to sell you only this type of policy, get a new agent who knows all of the insurance products and will sell you what you want and need, based on your specific circumstances. Note, however, that this is not a bad policy; if it is right for you, then buy it, but be advised on all the types of policies available before you make a decision.

NOTES TO SELF

UNIVERSAL LIFE

The universal life policy is much like the whole life policy, but the premiums are generally lower than those of the whole life, and the cash value of the policy grows slower. The features of both the whole life and the universal life policies are much the same. Many times an agent will place a customer in this policy in order to get the sale by offering a lower premium. The lower premium is enticing to the client, and the sale is made. The results of the illustration can vary greatly based on the projected rate of return. If the projected rate of return is too high, the results will be disastrous, the policy will not carry itself, and the policy will lapse, thus leaving the client with no insurance.

More universal life policies are being sold today than whole life policies. This is because this type of policy is a good, competitive policy. It performs well, and when coupled with a no lapse guarantee, it will be there when you need it.

NOTES TO SELF

VARIABLE UNIVERSAL LIFE

The variable universal life policy is the newest type of policy of those I've discussed. It is designed to buy insurance and at the same time purchase an investment, which, it is hoped, will grow big. The growth will increase the cash value, which will pay the premiums and increase the value of the policy. This type of policy is also sold by some as a retirement policy. When you retire, if the policy has grown as projected, you can borrow the cash value, tax free, and live off the borrowed proceeds.

Many agents sell only this type of policy, perhaps because of the large commissions generated. When purchasing this type of policy, you must be cautious. The investments are generally placed in a fund that is invested in equities in the form of mutual funds. You do not own mutual funds yourself; you only own an interest in the pool of funds. The pool owns the mutual funds. These equities are generally stocks in companies which are traded on the stock market. Thus, when the stock market goes down, so does the value of your investment and consequently the cash value of your policy. The risk in this type of policy is as great as the risk of buying your own stocks on the market. In many instances you may have to add amounts of money to the policy to keep it alive if it does not perform as projected or the stock market goes down. Be cautious when buying a variable universal life policy; you may be running with the big dogs.

NOTES TO SELF

SECOND TO DIE INSURANCE POLICY

This type of policy insures two people on the same policy, but it only pays out when the latter of the two people dies. It is used primarily for estate planning as a tool to pay costs of death or estate and inheritance taxes. This policy can also be used to create wealth for the next generation, as can most life policies.

The best way to describe this type of policy is with an example. Let's assume John and his wife have a large estate, which, after use of all estate planning tools, would require a one million dollar estate and inheritance tax payment. Rather than liquidate the assets to pay the taxes, John decides to obtain a Second to Die Insurance Policy to pay the taxes. This policy for the amount of one million dollars is on both John and his wife. It will pay the proceeds when John and his wife have both passed away. In order to not have the insurance policy included in his estate, thus resulting in more taxes, John places the insurance policy in a ILIT, otherwise known as a Irrevocable Life Insurance Trust. The Trust now owns the policy, and John's four children are the beneficiaries of the Trust. Upon the deaths of John and his wife, the one million dollars is paid to the Trust. Because it is not John's, it is not included in his estate, and no estate tax is due on the money. Furthermore, no income taxes are due on payment of the policy. The children now have the money tax free and can use it to pay the taxes on the estate without having to liquidate any of John's assets.

This type of policy is a good deal when used appropriately, and the best part about it is the price. Compared to the other types of life insurance, except Term Insurance, this is the least expensive. It is very cost efficient. However, in order to use this policy effectively, you must have a good estate attorney and a good insurance professional.

NOTES TO SELF

_____

_____

Note: *Generally, life insurance proceeds are not taxed as income! Talk to your CPA and insurance professional for details.*

LONG-TERM CARE INSURANCE

Over the last 20 years the complexity of our society has changed how we care for our elderly. In times past when a parent, or even a younger person, developed health problems, the families rallied together to provide for their needs. The trend today is to provide long-term care needs through the growing industry of health care facilities known as assisted living centers, nursing homes, or care centers. There are several reasons for this movement, among them three major reasons. First, it requires the income from both the husband and wife of many households to survive; thus no one is left home to provide for this care. Second, in many instances the health of the care giver has been destroyed in trying to provide for loved ones. An example of this occurs when a smaller partner continually has to lift a larger one. Third, in many instances the care at home simply is not of the quality the patient needs. The professional facility simply provides better care. Whatever the reason, these types of arrangements must be considered as you prepare for retirement.

In looking at this issue you should address several questions:

- What is your current health condition?
- Does your family have a history of some type of illness that must be considered?
- Will there be someone there to meet these needs?
- What will it cost to provide the needs?

Once you have answered the first three questions, the last question becomes of utmost importance.

The cost of what is termed "Long-Term Care" varies from state to state and city to city. Any way you look at it, the care is expensive. The rates average around $55,000 per year. Some states, like California, are more expensive. Whatever the rate, which will continue to increase at a very fast pace, the question is, how do we get this type of money? This is where Long-Term Care Insurance comes into play.

Long-Term Care Insurance is designed to pay the costs of a person being in a rest home. The policy has many variables, which can be included or left out. The main items to be considered are:

- How much money do I want the policy to pay per month, such as $1,000, $2,000 or more per month?
- How long do I want the policy to cover, such as one year, two years, or more?

- How long a waiting period do I want to wait before the policy pays?

These and other questions will get you started. You must consider this type of insurance, and you must know that the younger you are when you purchase this type of policy, the less expensive it will be.

Because of the high cost of Long-Term Care and all the heartaches it brings, this is probably a good place to give my philosophy of life and how to cope with the problem.

I believe that as you mature (a ten-dollar word for *get older*), you must run harder. You must never give up any of your physical abilities, like walking, running, swimming, biking, tennis, and so on. When you give them up, you lose them. You run harder and faster as you mature so that when you arrive at the pearly gates, or wherever you are going, you do it in a cloud of dust and skid fifteen feet. And hopefully, with luck, you will drop dead on the run, or at the hands of a jealous acquaintance. Either way, you will avoid the Long-Term Care center.

NOTES TO SELF

_____

_____

HEALTH INSURANCE

Health insurance is essential in our day. Medical costs are skyrocketing, and prospects are that they will continue to climb. It takes only one medical emergency, and the savings of a lifetime could be gone. Even worse, your earnings for many years to come could be diverted from your retirement planning. The following items need to be considered.

- When you are young you feel invincible—you know you will have no health problems, and you will live forever. When you get a family, even with only a spouse, you are subject to all the medical challenges that may come. One experience at the hospital can cost ten or twenty thousand dollars. Without insurance, this can really hurt. Recently a young acquaintance of mine who had been married for only three months had a heart attack. In the next two months his expenses were huge. In three months he passed away, and the young widow was left alone to cope with medical expenses of over $100,000. There was no medical or life insurance to help.

- Medical insurance can be provided by your employer. Medical insurance is very expensive, and if you can get insurance at your place of employment, get it. For those who cannot get insurance where they work, the cost is going to be high. Search around and do the best you can. It may even be to your advantage to change employment to a company where medical insurance is available. Then get it.

- My experience is that many people who are self-employed do not have health insurance. They look at the risk and the cost, and if profits are low, they take the chance. Most of these people pray a lot and hope for the best. I always recommend they get health insurance, but most do not. All I can say is "good luck."

- When a person retires, health insurance changes very fast. At retirement, most people are forced into the Medicare insurance program. I personally think the Medicare program is very poor. Some people are very fortunate to have insurance that carries on after retirement. They are most blessed. For those who do not, it is imperative to obtain a supplemental health insurance policy to pick up all of the medical expenses that Medicare does not cover. Most of the insurance companies that formerly provided insurance for retired people now provide this supplemental coverage. Get it. You cannot afford to be without it.

I believe one of the biggest challenges in life is to be able to grow old gracefully. Few there be that achieve it. The ravages of maturity and age-related ailments devastate many. The costs are even harder on you. You must have health insurance coverage to survive.

NOTES TO SELF

NOTE: When you retire, your exposure to risk in life generally lessens. A retired couple's greatest risk of liability is in three areas. You are personally liable for accidents that happen at your home, any accidents you have in your car, and medical expenses. You can protect from all of these types of liability through insurance. I recommend the following limits of liability to give you adequate protection in these areas.

HOME OWNERS POLICY

When you buy a home, if you have a mortgage or Trust Deed to secure the debt, the lender always requires home owners insurance during the term of the debt payment. Sometimes when the mortgage is paid in full, a home owner discontinues the home owner's liability policy. You should *never* discontinue your home owner's policy. The policy not only protects from liability of accidents, it also protects in the event of fire or other disasters that may occur to your home. Most insurance companies provide liability coverage, which is equal to the value of the home. In most instances this is adequate coverage for liability on your home. Your liability limit should never be less than $100,000.

NOTES TO SELF

_____

_____

AUTO POLICY

The liability for retired people is much higher for their automobile than for their home. There are more accidents in automobiles than in homes. However, I have found that most individuals are under-insured when it comes to their auto policy.

Many people tend to insure to the very minimum required under state law. I personally feel that a high liability coverage is the very best protection for a retired person. I have, over the years, recommended to my clients that the liability portion of their auto policy be a minimum of $300,000; ideally, it should be $500,000. When there is an accident with low liability limits, the insurance company will write a check and you are left to deal with any balance. If you have a high liability limit, you will get the very best protection and the best representation from your insurance company. I also recommend that property damage coverage be $100,000.

NOTES TO SELF

_____

_____

UMBRELLA POLICY

In the event you desire better coverage than that provided by your home owners and your auto policies, as discussed above, you can obtain what is called an Umbrella Policy. An umbrella policy is one that covers liability above and beyond your regular auto and home owners policies. If you have your home owners and your auto policy with the same company, you can likely obtain an umbrella policy fairly inexpensively, depending on where you live in the country. In my locality one can obtain a $1,000,000 umbrella policy for less than $200 per year. This gives you adequate protection in almost all circumstances.

NOTES TO SELF

_____

MEDICAL EXPENSES

The other area of large exposure for retired people is medical expenses. This is an enormous liability and continues to climb at ever-escalating rates. You must have health insurance coverage. Please see the section on Health insurance and Long-Term Care insurance for a complete discussion of these needs.

NOTES TO SELF

NOTE

I have always recommended that you have a good insurance professional working for you as you look toward retirement. In fact, you should get this person in place when you are young and work with him or her throughout your life. I also recommend that the person you choose be a member of a larger firm. He or she will have better knowledge and be better able to serve you. Independent agents generally are not as good at what they do.

Your insurance is much like homes and cars—you can buy too much home and you can buy too much car. You should be cautious when purchasing insurance that you do not buy more than you can afford or need. Some people refer to this as being insurance poor.

Finally, there are thousands of insurance companies and products to choose from. I recommend, when you buy an insurance product, that you obtain it from a good company that has high ratings in the insurance rating services. It would be tragic to buy a policy from an inferior company and not have the company be there when needed, and there be no money for the emergencies.

CHAPTER SIX

ASSISTED LIVING AND REST HOMES

WHO HELPS WHO

In past times in our society, when individuals matured and needed special care, the needs were met by family members. Most often a child would take a mother or a father into the home and care for them until the time of their demise. However, due to the changes in our society, that option is not always available in families. In many households everyone is working to provide for the daily living expenses and no one is left home who could care for a maturing parent. Thus our society is moving toward one in which the health care industry meets the demands for health care in a variety of medical institutions. We now have assisted living centers, rehabilitation centers, rest homes, care centers, day care centers, and a variety of other institutions to help care for the physical, mental and medical needs of our maturing population.

Although the race of life is an individual race, each runner is involved with many other runners. It is our interaction with those other runners which helps determine our success. It also helps determine the success of the other runners. This section discusses options for all runners in the race.

81

FAMILY ARRANGEMENTS

Family arrangements to care for the elderly can take many forms. The following information is designed to give you a feeling for what you can do to provide for those needs. You will need to work with family members and other professionals to determine what will be best for you. The three examples below illustrate some successful forms of family arrangements.

Mimi was 101 years old. She lived with family members and was still fairly active. Because of her age, the family she lived with did not like to leave her alone while they were at work during the day. In order to meet the needs of the family and not have Mimi feel she was a burden, the family hired a baby sitter to come in and watch Mimi's two-year-old great-granddaughter who lived in the home, thus also providing for Mimi and her needs.

Granny Wilcox stayed alone during the day. Family members sometimes brought in meals, and someone always stayed at her home during the nights. Sometimes this was a family member, sometimes a neighbor.

When my father became terminally ill with cancer, he wanted to stay in his own home. We all want to stay in our own homes. He lived there until the time he needed someone with him at all times to care for him. At that time I gave him his choice: either go to a hospital or a care center, or come live with me. This was a very emotional decision for him. He didn't want to go back to the hospital, so he chose to come and live with me. This was an enjoyable time for all our family members and a great blessing for my father. For those fortunate enough to be able to make these arrangements, I highly recommend it. The fact is that in our society, most people don't have this option.

_____

_____

ASSISTED LIVING CENTERS

Velda moved into an Assisted Living Center. She had her own two-room apartment, meals were provided in the cafeteria, church services were held each week, transportation was provided for shopping and medical visits or other desires, crafts were available, and group activities were provided. Employees were ever-present to check on her and provide for special needs. Velda loved her living conditions. The family lived close, visited her regularly, and were very happy with the way her needs were met.

There are many centers like this throughout the country. Some are very nice, and as long as the individual is ambulatory (able to move around), the centers provide very dignified living conditions. The cost for these centers varies widely, generally $2,000 to $4,000 per month. Given that all the meals, housecleaning and other needs are met, this is fairly reasonable.

As an individual's health declines, the person may need a higher level of care. Many of these centers have licenses to provide that care. For those who are in this type of a center, it is very convenient to change from one level of care to a higher level of care without disrupting or upsetting the individual. In those centers not licensed to provide additional care, the individual will be required to move to another type of facility as health deteriorates.

NOTES TO SELF

_____

_____

REHABILITATION CENTERS

Many times after people have suffered from a medical emergency, they are transferred into a rehabilitation center before they go home or to another type of facility. These centers are staffed by medical and rehabilitation specialists who work with patients to bring them back to a better state of health. For example, if individuals have suffered from a stroke, they may work with specialists to improve their speech, enable them to walk, dress themselves, feed themselves or meet other physical challenges. These centers generally are not designed for patients to stay for an extended period of time.

Many Rehabilitation Centers are combined with care centers or rest homes so that a patient can receive all the care needed without having to move to a new facility.

NOTES TO SELF

_____

_____

REST HOMES/CARE CENTERS

When a person's health deteriorates to the point he or she must have 24-hour supervision, rest homes (care centers) provide that care. The cost for these facilities runs around $5,000 or more per month. When selecting a facility for your loved ones, I offer the following pointers:

- Check on the cleanliness of the facility. Much can be determined by sight and smell.
- Check on the palatability of the food.
- Check on the credentials of the professional help.
- Check on how often professionals (doctors and nurses) visit with the patients.
- Check with other patients, or patients' families, to determine their satisfaction with the facility.
- Check on how friendly and personable the employees are.
- Before placing a family member in the facility, answer this question: "Would I be happy in this facility?"

Although we may have negative feelings about these types of institutions, they are essential in our society. All too often in an effort to care for an ailing family member, the health of the care giver is lost because of the physical demands of providing care for the ill person. Many very fine facilities in our country will help maturing individuals maintain their dignity and make them feel they are still important, despite their failing health. As you or family members mature, take some time to check with the professionals in your area to determine what type of an institution will best meet the needs of you or your loved ones. Growing old need not be a negative experience, and proper planning can keep a family close together under pleasant conditions.

NOTES TO SELF

MEDICARE

Medicare Insurance provides health insurance for aged or disabled people. Although the original concept was not to replace the existing insurance system, but to provide insurance for those who could not afford it, it didn't work out that way. Whenever you get the government involved in anything, it screws it up. As a result, most people, when they retire, have no choice but to go on Medicare Health Insurance. Most insurance companies provide only a supplement to the Medicare program after Social Security Retirement. If you are fortunate enough to have a health insurance provided through your employment after retirement, other than Medicare, count your blessings. Most people, when they retire, have no option other than to accept the Medicare program, which, in my humble but most thoughtful opinion, is a very poor program.

Medicare has two parts: Part A, hospital insurance; Part B, medical insurance. The program is administered by the Center for Medicare and Medicaid Services, a federal program.[8]

I offer several suggestions that may help in retirement planning.

- Because the Medicare program has very poor coverage, it is essential that you purchase a supplemental health program. These supplemental programs pick up the medical expenses where Medicare leaves off. They are offered by most insurances companies.

- Medicare provides few long-term care benefits. Therefore, when you go into a long-term care center, or rest home, you must pay all the costs for these services. Because the expenses are so high for long-term care, I recommend you look very carefully at long-term care insurance. This is discussed more completely under the section Long-Term Care, but you must know that at $4,000 to $5,000 per month, it doesn't take long to deplete your retirement savings.

- You must stay healthy. It is imperative that you enter into some form of a health and exercise program that will keep you as physically fit as possible. The statistics of many studies show that those who eat well and exercise regularly have a better quality of life with less illness. Therefore, to keep from using your Medicare insurance, eat healthfully and exercise (see the section Quality of Life).

- Look carefully at your spouse's work record before retiring. In many instances, the spouse does not have the required 40 quarters of employment to qualify for full Medicare Insurance or Social Secuirity benefits. This is a particular problem for those who are self-employed.

Spouses may put in many years of work in the business, but because they have not received a regular wage, they do not have the required 40 quarters to qualify for full benefits. This condition may arise when using a Limited Liability Company, a Sub-S Corporation, a Family Limited Partnership or a Sole Proprietorship. If you use any of these forms of business, you must start early to provide for spouse compensation if you intend to have full Social Security and Medicare coverage upon retirement. Although your spouse did not work enough to receive full Social Security Benefits, a stay-at-home spouse, or one who works in a family business without pay, can receive Social Security benefits based on the other spouse's qualification. The benefits are about one-half of what the qualifying person receives. If the qualifying person receives one thousand dollars, the non-qualifying spouse will receive about five hundred dollars. There are also Medicare benefits. Do not miss this benefit for retired persons.

NOTES TO SELF

_____

_____

_____

MEDICAID

Medicaid is a government program that will pay a person's medical expenses once all resources have been exhausted. In order to qualify for Medicaid, your assets will be reduced to $2,000 or less. There are many varying rules in order for a person to qualify for Medicaid. It is a federal program, administered through state agencies. There are exemptions for surviving spouses, for home, and for car. Because the program is administered by the individual states, the rules for qualification in your area may vary. I believe the Medicaid program is a last resort for those that have no other option and no other assets. You need to know that this program is available, and if you have no other alternatives, it can provide your medical care. There are professionals in your area who can assist you in deciding when and if you should apply for Medicaid.

You should note the following:

- Medicaid payments to or for you may become a lien upon your home or other assets.
- When you receive Medicaid payments, the program may take all of your Social Security or other retirement benefits.
- The worst thing to do is recover after you have qualified for Medicaid, because you are usually left a pauper with no assets.
- When you apply for Medicaid, whether you qualify or not usually depends on what the administrator you are dealing with had for breakfast.
- Because the amount paid for your care under Medicaid is limited, the care you generally receive under this program is of a lesser quality than that received when the payments for care are made through some other source.

The best thing to do when it comes to the Medicaid program is to develop a retirement program early in your life, one that provides for alternatives to the Medicaid program. Follow the plan consistently so that when you retire you will not have to become involved in this health care program.

_____

_____

HOSPICE

Hospice is a program administered to and for the benefit of persons who are terminally ill with a life expectancy of six months or less. A person can qualify for Hospice through Medicare, Medicaid, and most private insurances. This program is designed to provide care and comfort for those who are terminally ill and may be administered either at home or in care centers. Many times the care is administered by trained volunteers who work not only with the patient but with family members. The care can extend from patient needs to emotional and spiritual support for the family in preparation for the death of the patient.

It would be important for you to know about this program, not only for yourself, but for your parents or family and friends who may find themselves in need of Hospice. It has been my experience over the years that those who have benefited from this program have generally praised the care and treatment received. I recommend, if you have spare time, that you look at volunteering to work in the Hospice program. The challenges are many but the rewards are everlasting. Participation will also allow you to become familiar with the program should you have future need of it.

NOTES TO SELF

_____

PRESCRIPTIONS

If you have been to the pharmacy lately for a prescription, you have found the cost for such items is out of control. Recently a friend of mine, while being assessed $100 for a single pill, remarked, "At least Jessie James had a gun when he held up his victims." This may seem hilarious to those who do not need regular required prescriptions as a result of failing health, but the cost of prescriptions can not only cause you further health problems, it can bankrupt you in the process. The law passed in 2004 could offer some potential relief for this challenge. However, it appears that the program is not as effective as it was presented, and adequate relief does not appear to be forthcoming.

Within the United States there are places to obtain prescriptions through mail order services, generally at a lower price than you can get at your local pharmacy. I recommend that you talk to your family and friends, senior citizen groups, or others who can help you find a less expensive source for your prescriptions. However, be cautious when purchasing prescriptions outside the country; be sure you are dealing with a reputable source. Many senior citizens are filling their prescriptions in Mexico or Canada in order to overcome the high cost of prescription drugs. If this is the only way to get relief, go for it. It amazes me that one can get the same brand names of medicine in Mexico for a third or half the cost than in the United States. If you can use a generic drug rather than a brand name, it is generally less expensive.

The cost of prescriptions in retirement is a factor to consider. A health insurance program that pays for all or part of your prescriptions is a very good deal. When you sign up for supplemental health insurance, this is an item you will want to examine very closely.

Good food and good exercise may be a good alternative to the high cost of prescription drugs.

NOTES TO SELF

_____

_____

WINNING OR LOSING

The information contained in this book is of such importance that it needs to be shared with Family and Friends. Additional copies may be obtained by visiting our website at: **winningorlosing.com**, or the publishers website at: **deverepublishing.com**. If you prefer you may also send the following order form directly to the publisher.

ORDER FORM

Please send me _____ copies of **WINNING OR LOSING** at the price of $24.95 each and no charge for shipping and handling (Utah residence include $1.60 state sales tax). My check or money order for $_____ is enclosed made payable to Devere Publishing.

Name_____

Address_____

City/State/Zip_____

Phone(____) _____   Fax(___) _____

E-mail_____

Send order to: Devere Publishing Inc.
　　　　　　　P O Box 970965
　　　　　　　Orem, UT 84097-0965

　　　　　　　Please allow 15 days for delivery
Additional copies may also be obtained by visiting your local bookstore.

96

CHAPTER SEVEN

ESTATE PLANNING

IF YOU'RE DEAD, YOU LOSE

At some point in the race of life you will pass the baton to the next generation. You may have noticed that this race of life went on before you were born and will continue after you die. A portion of your success of winning the race is to make provisions for the next generation to do well in their race as they continue after your demise. Hence, estate planning.

When I hear someone say, "Estate Planning" or "I want to do my Estate Planning," I become very nervous. The reason is that the term *Estate Planning* has many different meanings. To an attorney it means Wills and Trusts, to an insurance man it means insurance and annuities, to a tax man it means 401(k)'s and IRA's, and to a financial advisor it is all about investments. If you have not determined from reading this book that estate planning involves all of these things, let me emphasize that estate planning involves everything discussed in this book. Retirement Planning also involves everything discussed in this book. For purposes of presenting material in an organized manner, this chapter discusses legal items that should be addressed by your attorney. That includes Wills, Trusts, Living Wills, Medical Powers of Attorney, and General Durable Powers of Attorney. Some other legal documents may be prepared by the attorney because of special needs. They may be alluded to in this book, but only you and your attorney can determine what they are. If you fail to do proper estate planning, you will lose the race.

WILLS

Many times I am asked the question, "Can I do my own Will?" The answer to this is yes. There are books in the bookstore and in the library to tell you how to do this. There are books with Will forms where you fill in the blanks. I do not recommend you do your own Will. I have seen many Wills prepared from forms obtained in books. Very few of these are filled out correctly, most have missing information, and many are filled out with pencil. Any of these practices may render your Will invalid. When you die, you will have no opportunity to come back and correct those errors. I strongly recommend you go to an attorney and obtain a Will that is proper for your Estate Plan (see the section Selecting a Professional).

There are many types of Wills: Sweetheart or I Love You Wills, Pourover Wills for Trusts, Wills that create a Testamentary Trust, and so on. Which of these types is best for you depends on your specific situation, and only your attorney can determine which is best.

You should have a Will. Even if you have a Trust, you must have a Will to support that Trust. If you have minor children and need to name a Guardian, it must be done in your Will. That is the proper place for the naming of a Guardian (see the Section Guardians). In the event you do not have a Will, your possessions

will pass to your heirs under the laws of Intestate Succession. This means the State will determine who will inherit your possessions. State laws allow you to have a Will and name who will receive your estate. In the event you fail to do this, the state will determine your heirs. Having a Will and Trust becomes critically important if you have a second marriage, children with special needs, or other circumstances that need attention. Do yourself a favor by having a Will and Trust drafted by an attorney.

NOTES TO SELF

TRUSTS

Trusts seem to be a buzz word in our society. It was not always so. When I first started as an Estate Tax Attorney for the IRS, only the wealthy had Trusts. Most medium and small-size estates were passed to the heirs by a Will through Probate. However, wealthy clients had Trusts that were administered without Probate to pass their estate to their heirs. So what is a Trust? Is it better than just a Will? How does it work?

A Trust can be several things, but for purposes of this discussion, let us limit it to a basic Estate Planning tool. A Trust is a legal entity created by one or more individuals to hold and manage assets. It is administered by one or more Trustees for one or more beneficiaries. An example: The John and Mary Doe Trust, with John and Mary Doe Trustees, for the benefit of John and Mary Doe, while they are alive. This is a great simplification for a 12- to 15-page document. However, if you put your names in the place of John and Mary Doe, you will see that a basic Grantor Trust can be created for you and your spouse with you and your spouse as Trustees, and with you and your spouse as beneficiaries during your lifetime. Upon your deaths, the Trustee then distributes to your heirs the assets held in the Trust, as specified in the Trust Document.

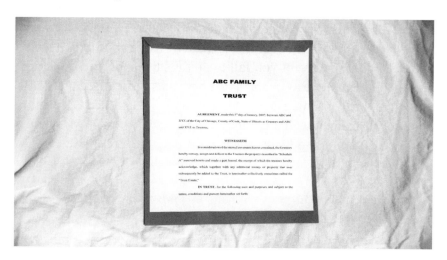

The benefit of a basic Grantor Trust over just a Will is that a Trust does not have to be probated. To probate a Will you must have an attorney, pay court fees, pay attorney fees, wait for time limitations to pass, notify creditors, become a public record, and hope it will all be done in a year. All the cost, time and hassle of Probate can be eliminated by the use of a Trust. I almost always recommend a Trust of some type; it is the best Estate Planning tool available in our society today.

There are many types of Trusts. Most people in our society do not need a complicated Trust. If your estate is small to medium size, a Grantor Trust is sufficient. If your estate is in a taxable category, you may need a Marital Deduction Trust or an Asset Protection Trust. The nature of the Trust you need will depend on where you live. For example, if you live in a Community Property State, your Trust will be different than if you live in a Common Law State or a Commonwealth State. Because of the variations of state laws, it is imperative that an attorney draft your Trust. Do not be misled by books that have Trust forms, or people who are not attorneys who market Trust forms or sell Trusts. The books you can buy in the bookstores with Trust forms are very complicated and hard to understand and hard to complete. In my legal experience I have never seen a Trust form from one of these books which was filled out properly, and I have spent a great deal of time correcting problems they have created.

Because of the variation and complication of Trusts, consider the following items when you create a Trust for your Estate Planning.

- Is your estate subject to estate, transfer, succession, legacy, inheritance or similar taxes, either federal or state?
- Do you have children or grandchildren who have special needs because of mental or physical handicaps?
- Is this a second marriage for either spouse?
- If this is a second marriage for either spouse, do you have a Pre-nuptial Agreement?

- Is one spouse much older than the other?
- Do you have minor children?
- Do you have business interests? (Partnership, LLC, Sub S Corporation, etc.)
- Do you have a Buy-Sell Agreement?
- Do you have a potential liability exposure?
- Do you have creditor problems?

A Trust can provide solutions to all these challenges, but they must be revealed to the attorney in order for him or her to make correct decisions. Once you have created the Trust, the following items are extremely important.

- All assets must be transferred into the Trust. A Trust that is not funded is worthless because your estate will have to be probated in order to get the assets into the Trust.

- Some attorneys do not help you transfer assets into the Trust. If this is the case, fire your attorney and find one who will help you properly place your assets into your Trust.

- Do not place IRAs or 401(k)s in a Trust, or make your Trust the beneficiary of IRAs or 401(k)s unless you are specifically advised to do so by your attorney and CPA. Making the Trust the owner or beneficiary of IRAs and 401(k)s has significant tax consequences and should not be done without the assistance and direction of your CPA.

- Real estate should be deeded into the Trust, and the deed should be recorded in the County Recorder's Office where the Property resides.

- If the Trust is intended to hold your business interest, such as LLC, Partnerships and/or Sub S Corporations, the evidence of ownership (stock or certificate) must be transferred to show the Trust as owner.

Many other types of Trust can be used for your benefit if the need exists. ILIT, QTIP, Generation Skipping and Irrevocable Trusts are specialty items that can be used, but they must be drafted by a very knowledgeable attorney.

NOTES TO SELF

_____

_____

_____

POWER OF ATTORNEY

A Power of Attorney is a legal document in which you give to another person the legal right to act for and in your behalf in almost all matters. This includes buying and selling things, control over financial matters, transferring assets, and many other actions. Because of the extensive legal rights given to another person in a Power of Attorney, you should be extremely cautious in making the decision to give this power. The most common uses for the Power of Attorney are between a husband and wife or a parent and child. When a spouse is being shipped overseas in the military, many times a Power of Attorney is given to a spouse who is staying home in order to transact all business in the absence of the partner. In some units of the military the JAG Corp may help prepare this document. Another common use for the Power of Attorney is between husband and wife, particularly when one of them develops physical or mental challenges that render them unable to function normally.

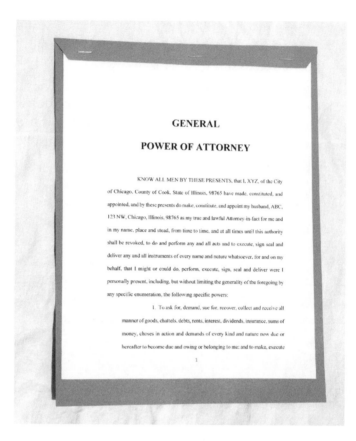

Two types of Powers of Attorney are generally used. One is a General Power of Attorney, the other a General Durable Power of Attorney. The difference between these two documents is that a General Power of Attorney normally ceases upon the incapacitation of the person giving the Power of Attorney. A General Durable Power of Attorney continues to function in spite of the disability of the individual. There are also special and limited Powers of Attorney. Do not prepare and sign any Powers of Attorney without being advised by your attorney on the legal implications.

NOTES TO SELF

LIVING WILLS

A Living Will is a document that provides a person who is terminally ill the choice to not be put on artificial life support systems and be kept alive above and beyond a natural death. Many people do not want to be kept in the hospital at great expense to their family. Forms for creating these documents are usually state-specific. Each state has its own forms. You should use the form from the state where you reside. Failure to do so may render your document inoperative in your state, and your desires may not be carried out.

With the medical technology currently available, bodily functions can be maintained even when the brain has ceased to function. Many individuals do not want this to happen. Many people feel that the use of these methods would tend to consume all the assets in their estate and leave nothing for survivors. The feelings and emotions involved in making a decision of this magnitude are deep. You must communicate with family members in making such a decision. You should also obtain a copy of the form used in your state and seek professional help so that you understand the implications of these documents.

If your feelings are as stated in the Living Will you must make this known by signing the document. Failure to execute a Living Will properly generally means the doctor is the one who makes the decision, not family members. The living Will must be made available to family members. If they cannot find it, they cannot use it.

A Living Will is extremely important in those circumstances where accidents may render a person into a vegetative state. The Terri Schiavo case is a prime example of a person being kept alive for many years in a vegetative state because that person did not have a Living Will and Medical Power of Attorney signed prior to the accident. The family members fought over the final outcome of

Terri's existence. The expense and hatred generated in this case destroyed any potential family relationship for the future. Not only did it affect the family, it became a national issue. In order to prevent these types of challenges, you must have your Living Will and Medical Power of Attorney filled out and properly signed.

NOTES TO SELF

_____

_____

MEDICAL POWER OF ATTORNEY

The Medical Power of Attorney, much like the Living Will, is a form specifically designed by each state. This document tells who should make medical decisions for and in your behalf if you are unable to do so. These documents usually specify a spouse or a family member to make medical decisions. For example, I have designated my wife to make medical decisions for me if I cannot. On the other hand, my wife has designated that I should make medical decisions for her in the event she is unable to.

It is extremely important that you have in your legal documents a Medical Power of Attorney. This document which designates someone to make medical decisions for you is directly related to the Terri Schiavo case. In that case no one was designated to make her medical decisions; therefore, her husband and her parents fought for many years over the medical directions for and in her behalf. To avoid this problem, make sure you have the form for your specific State properly filled out and made available to the designated person and family members.

When you sign this type of document I recommend that you be very careful to designate a person who understands your feelings and is able to carry out your wishes. Some family members become so emotional over medical challenges that they cannot make proper decisions. Some simply cannot pull the plug when it is time to go.

NOTES TO SELF

_____

_____

GUARDIANS

Many years ago, I witnessed a vicious court battle among family members over who would be the guardian of children of a deceased relative. To avoid such distasteful experiences, you must designate the guardian, and keep the documents updated as necessitated by changes which come along as a result of fluctuations in needs and values. The choosing of guardians is one of the most important decisions to be made when doing an estate plan. If you have minor children, it may be the most important decision you make. I have been known to be highly opinionated in this matter; therefore, I offer the following items and explanations for your consideration.

- The selection of the guardian is the most important decision you can make, and therefore it should be the very best choice you make. Many times people will appoint a guardian, not based on who would do the best job, but because they do not want to hurt someone's feelings. I do not believe in such a decision. The decision should be who will do the very best job at being guardian of your children in the event of your untimely demise.

- Many times individuals select their parents as guardians of their minor children. Although this is a great compliment to parents who have done a wonderful job of raising their children, I normally do not recommend you select your parents as guardians. My reasoning for this is as follows. When parents have raised their family it is extremely difficult for them to move back into the young-child stage. It becomes very difficult for them to keep up with the demands of a much younger and active generation. Several years ago, when my wife and I went to Hawaii to a conference, my wife's mother, who loves our children a great deal, consented to tend our children while we were away for ten days. My wife's mother had not had young children at home for a number of years, and the stress of trying to deal with a number of young children was huge. In fact, she returned to her own home three times during the ten-day period to seek some relief from the stress she was feeling.

- Many times individuals pick siblings, brothers and sisters as guardians—an excellent choice. However, please note that if family members are living a life style which does not meet with your requirements, do not hesitate to go outside the family relationship to find a guardian for your children.

- I always give my clients the following example when selecting guardians. If a child is placed with a person who has a college education, generally that child will follow suit and gain a college education. If a child is placed with someone who hunts and fishes, generally that child will follow the same and pursue these sports. If a child is placed with someone who smokes or drinks, that child will probably adopt these habits. So when selecting a guardian for your children, select one who will raise them in the manner you want them raised, according to your value system.

- I do not recommend that the guardian of your children and the Trustee of your Trust be the same individual. The guardian should be the person who has the care and keeping of your child or children and raises them as you want them raised. The Trustee should be the person who manages the Trust, invests it and guarantees that the funds will be there for your child's, children's and the guardian's use. By providing that these individuals not be the same person, you have a check and balance so you don't generate a conflict of interest.

NOTES TO SELF

_____

_____

_____

TRUSTEES

The selection of Trustee is an extremely important decision when creating a Trust. With most Trusts the Grantors, those creating the Trust are the initial Trustees. They control and manage Trust assets. The challenge generally comes in determining who should manage Trust assets upon the incapacitation or death of the Grantors.

The first choice, for many, is family members. Normally, younger couples will select parents. Parents generally have the ability to manage assets and money. The selection of parents may work well with younger couples, but as the parents mature or pass away, new Trustees will have to be selected. The second choice would be brothers and sisters or married children. This choice, however, may create conflict with the selection of Guardians. The third choice would be professionals or financial institutions.

Many times the individual you desire to be the Guardians for the children is also the individual you would choose for Trustee. It is important that the Trustee and Guardian not be the same individual. The Trustee's responsibility is money management. The Guardian's responsibility is caring for, loving and teaching the child. By selecting a different individual for each of these positions, you create a check and balance whereby there is no conflict of interest by serving in both capacities.

If you find that family members are not capable of managing their own assets, do not believe they will do better in managing Trust assets. There are many professionals who can manage Trust assets for and in behalf of your children. Look at banks, CPAs, or attorneys to fill the position of Trustee. Each will charge a fee for the service. However, it is better to pay a fee and maintain the assets than get a free service from family members and have no assets for your children. Do not worry about hurt feelings of family members in making this choice. You only get one shot at doing it right.

The following questions can assist you in the selection of Trustees:

FOR INDIVIDUALS AS TRUSTEE

- How do they manage their own finances?
- Have they filed bankruptcy?
- Have they ever managed anything other then a checking and savings account?
- Do they have a financial background in stocks, bonds, or other investments?
- Do they have moral values? Are they honest?
- Are they much older than you?
- Can they work well with the Guardian?

- Can they say no to requests for distributions for improper purposes?
- Do they like your children?

FOR FINANCIAL INSTITUTIONS AS TRUSTEE

- Do they have a Trust department?
- Are they licensed to do business as a Trustee?
- Are they bonded?
- Are they insured?
- How long has their Trust department been in operation?
- What is their credit rating?
- What is the experience level of their professionals?
- Where do they invest Trust funds?
- What is their investment history?
- What is the investment rate of return?
- How much do they charge for their services?
- How stable is the Trust department?
- Do they have a big turnover in employees?
- What is their reputation in the community?

It is important that you have the power to change Trustees. Times and circumstances and people change. If you find you need to change the Trustee, do it immediately. If you find you are dead and the Trustee needs to be changed, you have missed your chance. Your attorney should have made provisions for changing trustees when he or she drafted your Trust.

NOTES TO SELF

_____

_____

SECOND MARRIAGES

Over my many years of doing estate planning, the number of instances in which one or both of the spouses have been previously married has increased dramatically. Not only have I seen a large increase in second marriages at younger ages, but because people are living much longer, I have seen a dramatic increase in the second marriage of retired people after the loss of a spouse. In either instance, there are dramatic challenges when putting two families together. Without in-depth planning and the assistance of financial and legal professionals, the result of second marriages can be catastrophic for the families of both spouses. Each of us is familiar with cases where families have lost their inheritance to a new spouse, where children have destroyed the marriage over material concerns, or when the marriage did not work out, and the expense to one or both parties was devastating. In order to avoid and control such situations, I offer the following items which must be dealt with in second marriages:

- I have always recommended that a Prenuptial Agreement be signed by both parties of the marriage prior to the second marriage. An attorney can provide a Prenuptial Agreement.

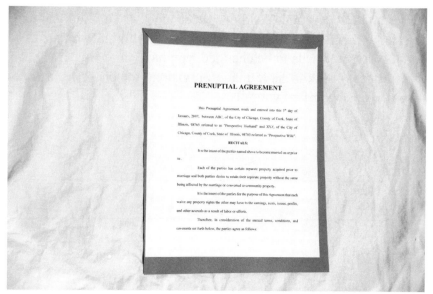

- Each party signing a Prenuptial Agreement must have their own attorney to give them independent legal advice. Don't share attorneys.

- Don't talk yourself into believing that if you really love him or her, you won't ask him or her to sign a Prenuptial Agreement.

- When you sign a Prenuptial Agreement, tell your children you have done so and that the Prenuptial Agreement has protected their inheritance. This should reassure the children and thus provide the opportunity for a much happier marriage.

- If the marriage does not work out, a Prenuptial Agreement will protect the estate of each individual from a divorce fight.

- If one spouse is younger than the other, life insurance or an annuity can be used to provide for the younger spouse during his or her lifetime should they survive the older spouse.

- Trusts can be used to protect estates, provide for surviving spouses, and meet the needs of distribution to children of previous marriages. You will need an attorney to draft these documents. Trust forms are not designed to meet these types of special needs.

- Sometimes it is best to move to *our home* rather than live in *my home* or *your home.*

NOTES TO SELF

_____

_____

CHILDREN WITH SPECIAL NEEDS

Many people have members of the family who are in a position that requires special provisions for them. These challenges are the result of accidents and birth defects in the form of mental or physical disabilities. The parents, generally, are the ones to provide for all of the needs of these individuals. If we retire on less income than we had when working full-time, or if we die, we must provide for these people.

One method to provide for these individuals is to create a Special Needs Trust. An attorney will be needed to create this Trust. The Trust is one in which funds are held for the benefit of the disabled person. It provides that the principal and income can be used for the person as determined by the Trustee. Special provision in this Trust must be used to protect the Trust assets from being taken over by governmental agencies that become involved in the care of the disabled. These Trusts can be funded by assets or life insurance. You should consult with professionals if you have this type of need.

Many government agencies provide programs to assist disabled persons. Many do a wonderful job. My only caution is to make sure that the needs of your family member are being met. Make sure the person is loved and properly supervised. If you want to provide for a disabled person and there is a government agency involved, be sure to consult an attorney for a Special Needs Trust.

NOTES TO SELF

_____

_____

GREED AND SPOUSE INFLUENCE

I have found that two things continually plague us as we mature. The first is *Greed*, the second *Spouse Influence*.

When our children are young, we watch them grow and develop, and generally we get to a point where we can fairly well predict what that child will do in a given set of circumstances. For example, if you give your children some candy, you will know which one will immediately devour every piece of candy you have given him or her. On the other hand, you know which child will hide it away for weeks, months or years so he or she will have it when it's wanted. An unpredictable trait is greed. Sometimes greed shows up in the most unexpected individuals as they mature, often on the death of the parents. For the first two days after the death of the parents, the children get along very well. By the time of the funeral, a few indications of conflict begin to arise among the children. When the children meet to divide personal property, greed comes out in its full, ugly confrontation over items of little financial worth but high sentimental value. I don't have an answer to solving this problem, but a couple of recommendations may help.

- Identify items of deep sentimental value, such as family antiques or heirlooms.
- Specify which items you want to go to each child.
- Write these decisions down and incorporate them in your Will and Trust (your attorney can help you with this).
- Tell your children what you have done and why, but at that point do not be specific as to who gets what, just that it is done.

The second item, Spouse Influence, is more subtle and difficult to deal with. Have you noticed that although you can predict exactly what a child will do under given circumstances, when that child marries, things change. This I call "Spouse Influence." It comes when two people marry and try to create one lifestyle. We all go through this. I feel I was very successful, and you may feel the same way. However, I am sure there were days when my parents felt like pounding their heads on the wall, saying, "What is that stupid kid doing?" Spouse Influence is not always bad; in fact, many times it is very beneficial. It improves our children a great deal as they mature. We may already know how the spouse influence will affect our children. Others of our children are either not married or they are young and not of marrying age. Because of the unknown results of spouse influence, let me offer a couple of suggestions to better cope with it and get better results.

- When you have family decisions to make, let your children's spouses know of those decisions, but do not let them participate in the decision making.
- Do not permit spouses of your children to alienate the children from the family.
- Do not alienate the spouses of your children.
- When your administrator or Trustee makes distribution of personal property and estate after your death, have only your children present. Do not permit spouses or others to attend.

116

These suggestions are somewhat idealistic. They may or may not work, but you must be aware of these potential problems and plan for them. If you do, things will definitely be much better than if these problems are ignored. As a final note, it is important that you love your children and their spouses and continually communicate with them. When you lose the ability to communicate, you lose the ability to solve the problems that will arise as a result of the life process (daily living). When you retire it would be terrible to be all alone if you have alienated your children and their spouses and no one wants to come and see you

NOTES TO SELF

_____

_____

DISINHERITANCE

Sometimes in life, our children don't rise to the level of our expectations. When my first child was born, I expected she would be the most nearly perfect child that ever lived. As a parent, I knew everything there was to know about raising children. When the second child came along, I had to revise all my theories, because she didn't match what I thought was my perfect program for raising children. When the third and fourth children came along, all my knowledge for raising children and what they would be was in mass disarray. When I was twenty, I knew all the questions and answers about raising children. At age forty, I knew the questions but I didn't have any answers. At age fifty I didn't know the questions or answers. Now in my mature years and as I look back at the lessons my children have taught me, I realize a couple of extremely important lessons.

- I realize that every child is an individual; no two are alike. Therefore my expectations for what my children should

117

become were probably of no value. Realizing that each one is an individual and each has the freedom to choose what he or she will become in life adds to the uniqueness of each child.

- Each child is unique among all other persons on the earth. I should not expect a child to fit into a mold I had designed in my mind as to what constituted his or her success or failures in life.

- I realize that even when my child made decisions which I probably would not make, it is still my obligation and responsibility to love that child for who he or she is.

- My responsibility was to teach my children honesty, integrity, and charity, and to do good to all men. If children live these principles, they can be successful in anything they choose because they will be happy and content with themselves.

Now, to the subject at hand, *disinheritance*. I have had clients ask if they could disinherit a child for various reasons. One client wanted to disinherit a daughter because she was going to get a divorce, and he didn't believe in divorce. He had no idea what she had to endure or what injustices were imposed upon her, only that Dad didn't believe in divorce. I have heard few dumber things. Divorces are the most devastating legal action a person can deal with. Divorce causes an individual to question values, integrity and self-worth. In these instances, children need all the love and support you can give them.

I have never recommended that a parent disinherit a child. Even though a child may do some things to displease you, I believe it is a parent's responsibility to still love and teach and pray for the benefit of their children, even when they do stupid things. I also believe there is nothing more important on this earth than family. It has been my experience that if a child is disinherited, it will destroy the relationship between the child and parent, which relationship can never be reclaimed in this life. The fractured relationship will carry on from generation to generation, and family unity will suffer.

I believe that when children have done something to displease you, rather than disinherit them, continue to love them and to teach them. If you destroy the relationship, you will lose the ability to communicate with, teach or guide a child, and you will never be able to help the child change. Disinheritance always destroys relationships. If you have a child who has made some bad choices and has a special problem that upsets you, such as being a spendthrift or using drugs, see your attorney. An attorney can place provisions in a Trust that will provide for the child, yet not support the habits, without disinheritance.

NOTES TO SELF

_____

_____

CHAPTER EIGHT

FAMILY

SCORING BONUS POINTS

Nothing in this world is more important than family relations. Family includes parents, siblings, spouse, children, grandchildren and great-grandchildren. When it comes to the race of life, this group of individuals will define your success in everything you do. Failure in any of these relationships cannot be compensated for by your success in business, sports, or other pursuits.

PARENTS

The Lord stated in the Ten Commandments (Exodus 20:12), "Honour thy father and thy mother: that thy days may be long upon the land which the LORD thy God giveth thee." It has always been of interest to me that this scripture states that *Thy*, not your parents', but *your* days may be long upon the land, by honoring your mother and father. Your parents have brought you into this life. They teach, train and care for you. They clothe, feed and educate you and prepare you to take your place in society. For this you should be grateful. When your parents get more mature, it should be your responsibility to give to them the same care they were so dedicated giving to you.

I know children do not always agree with their parents. As individuals, we each have the ability and responsibility to make our own choices and decisions, which are never the same for any two of us. However, just because I do not cut the lawn the same way, decorate my house the same, like the same make of car or like or dislike the Dallas Cowboys, there is no reason I cannot honor and respect my parents. Sometimes we let little things become huge barriers in our relationship with our parents. I had a client who had not communicated with his parents for over twenty years because of an argument over a shotgun. How lame is that?

To honor our parents may take many courses. My friend Steve has lived with and provided for his mother for many years. He has done everything for her because she did not want to go to a rest home. This care is twenty-four hours a day, seven days a week, and in her failing health he does for her all the things she did for him when he was a baby. You may not be required to give this type of service. But some people don't even visit their parents, or say thank you, or call them on the phone. As I have said before, what goes around comes around, and some day you will mature and be one of the older generation. I hope you receive the same type of honor from your children that you have given to your parents.

NOTES TO SELF

SPOUSE

When I ask the question "Why did you marry your spouse?" I always get the same answer: "Because I loved her and wanted to be with her." That is why I married my wife, Peggy. As soon as we got married, other things started to interfere with my marriage relationship. My boss required that I put in up to ten hours a day at work. The college professors required that I attend class and do my studies. When the children came along, they demanded a lot of time. My career required that I do certain things in order to succeed, and there were a hundred other things, when I allowed them, which would interfere with my relationship with my spouse. I had to make a conscious decision to keep my wife as the most important priority in my life. All the important things in my life had to be prioritized, but I had to keep my spouse as my number-one priority.

There is nothing or anyone that is more important than your spouse!

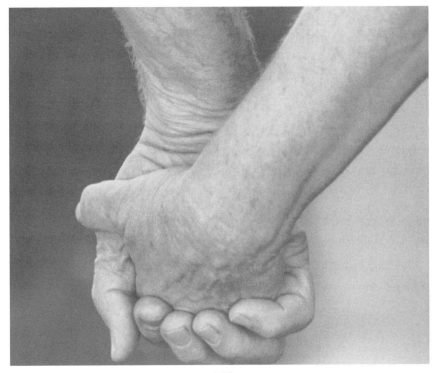

Many in our society have different opinions. All are entitled to their own opinion, even when they are wrong. This book is about retirement, and there is nothing more rewarding in retirement than sharing it with a spouse with whom you have developed a relationship over the last forty or fifty years. The most miserable people I have met, although healthy both physically and mentally, are those who did not develop the relationship with their spouse and consequently spent retirement alone.

Younger people in our society seem to have a philosophy of waiting until twenty-five, thirty or forty to get married, and if for some reason it doesn't work out, get a divorce and try again. In my day, we married at a younger age and grew up together. When things were tough, we worked it out together. Those who have not had this opportunity do not comprehend what they have missed. It is kind of like a man describing birthing labor to women: men don't have the background or experience to express what is involved. So it is with marrying and growing old with your spouse. This experience is the greatest and most fulfilling you can ever have, but those who don't experience it will not understand what they have missed.

Those who are not married or are divorced tend to criticize marriage. I believe married people are happier, live longer, have better physical and mental health, and perform better in the business world. If you are having a bad experience in marriage, don't give up; you still have time to correct the marriage relationship. It would be advisable to seek marriage counseling from your clergy or a professional marriage counselor. If you have gone through a divorce, learn from the experience; you can remarry and build a very healthy marriage relationship, but use different techniques and priorities than you did with your first marriage.

In order to maintain your marriage relationship, you can do many things. Let me recommend a few:

- Continue to date your spouse on a regular basis.
- Do special things for your spouse without a reason.

- Take time each day to talk when the children are not present.
- Make goals and plans together.
- Solve problems together.
- Take special trips together.
- Don't let the children separate or divide you. You were together before they came, you will be together after they go.
- Always say you are sorry even when you are not wrong.
- Attend a church of your choice together.
- Never go to bed angry or upset with each other. Solve problems daily.
- Never turn your attention or affection to another person.
- Never let your profession interfere with the marriage relationship.
- Work hard, have a budget and stay out of debt. Bad finances destroy marriages.
- Say, "I Love You!" often.

Someone told me, years ago, that if I kissed my wife every time I left the house, I would live ten years longer than men who don't kiss their wives every time they left the house. I don't know if this is true or not, but I do know it has improved our relationship. It has been worth it to drive around the block and come back to the house when I have forgotten to kiss my wife. And if I live ten years longer, great! The point is this: you do whatever you need to do to improve your relationship with your spouse.

It is a known fact that we all mature, and we all die. In most instances a husband and wife do not pass away at the same time. One is left alone, and the loneliness is a terrible experience. Many times the children of the marriage oppose a single parent remarrying. However, I recommend that if you find someone in the same situation as you, with whom you are compatible, marry them. There is nothing worse than the loneliness after the loss of a spouse. Children should continue to love and support their parents when the parents make a decision to remarry. When considering a second marriage, be sure to read the section in this book on Second Marriages.

NOTES TO SELF

_____

_____

_____

CHILDREN

Children are an absolute necessity in life. If it were not so, you and I would not be here. There are those who choose not to have children or who limit their families to one or two children. That is there choice. Peggy and I have a large family, by choice, and I have found each child to be different and unique. You have probably found the same thing in your family. There is nothing as cute and cuddly as a six-month-old baby, nor is there anything as unpredictable and complex as a teenager. Some people succeed at conquering mountains. I was grateful to have survived the teenage years. Our children were not bad children, they were just busy and energetic, and the girls were emotional. Raising our children has been one of the greatest highlights of our life.

Children, whether they are a babe in arms or eighty years old, should be loved by their parents. They should be allowed to make their choices and suffer the consequences of those choices. They should be loved, taught, encouraged and praised. They should not be abused, harmed or criticized, but they should be corrected when they make mistakes. When children do something stupid, and they will, you still need to love them. When they do things different than you, and they will, ask yourself if it really matters that they

126

did it differently. The first time I asked one of my sons to mow the lawn, he did it in such a pattern as to leave squares, triangles, rectangles and circles in unusual places. It drove me nuts. I simply asked, "Are you through?" and then watched. When he was finished it looked great. Even though he had done it different than I would, it didn't matter. The job was done, and I didn't need to criticize or correct him.

Whatever your children need to do, let them do it their way and give them encouragement as long as it is not harmful or is not a moral issue. Those of us who are more mature have witnessed the greatest changes the world has ever known. Our children are geniuses. They talk in languages that are foreign to us. They perform tasks not even thought of when we were young. You can learn much from your children. I rely regularly on my children to teach and help me in things beyond my training.

I believe that in addition to loving and caring for our children, we must train them to take their place in society. They will be the next leaders of our nations and countries. We should instill in them the religious and moral values by which to govern future societies.

NOTES TO SELF

GRANDCHILD AND SO FORTH

It is a great experience to be a grandparent. When grandchildren are wet, you give them to their mother. When they are hungry, you give them to their mother. When they cry, you give them to their mother. You can cuddle, hug, play with and spoil your grandchildren and then send them home with their parents. Grandchildren are full of energy—they wear you out, they go in circles, they make lots of noise, and sometimes it is nice to see the taillights on the car when their parents take them home. Have you noticed how nice the silence is after the grandchildren have visited?

Along with all of the benefits of being a grandparent, there remain some grave responsibilities which only a grandparent can fill. Although we do not have the responsibility to care for all the immediate needs of grandchildren, we still have a lot that can benefit them. I believe we must set a proper example for them— in values, in education, in recreation, in religion, and in family relationships. Many times a grandparent's advice will be listened to by teenages when parents have no ability to communicate with them. Grandchildren will often watch what a grandparent does and follow that example.

Here are several suggestions that will help maintain a relationship with grandchildren.

- Visit them as often as possible.
- Give little gifts—they mean as much as big gifts.
- Attend their school and church programs as often as possible.
- Listen to their accomplishments and ideas.
- Go on trips and outings with them.
- Don't tell the same boring stories over and over again.
- Praise them.
- Love them even when they seem to be unlovable.

Not many years from the time you become a grandparent, you will become a great- grandparent. The same rules and responsibilities you have as a grandparent will apply to each succeeding generation you are privileged to know. Let me recommend you write your own history. Then your future generations, which come after you are gone, may still be influenced by your life.

NOTES TO SELF

_____

_____

_____

FUNERALS

One of the most stressful times in life is when loved ones pass away. Not only is it stressful because of the loss of someone you are close to, but I have found it is extremely stressful from a financial point, because of the cost of funeral and burial plans. Over the years I have seen funerals that range from extremely expensive, $20,000 to $30,000, to inexpensive funerals, where loved ones are laid to rest in a pinewood box. You should consider the options at least by the time of retirement. When proper plans are made and put into effect, the loss of a family member can be one of celebrating the life of a great individual rather than worrying about medical and funeral expenses. Because of the potential extreme stress, I offer the following items for consideration.

- It is a fact of life that all of us are going to die; no one lives forever. You need to know that death is as much a part of life as birth.

- A funeral costs as much as a birth. Normally we pay for a birth through health insurance, and there are plans that will help pay for a funeral. These funeral plans can be obtained at almost all mortuaries. If you have not made other provisions, you may want to look into these types of plans.

- Many individuals purchase a life insurance policy designed specifically to pay for final medical expenses and funeral expenses. These policies can be obtained from most insurance companies. I recommend that these policies be for an amount between $15,000 and $20,000. If you need insurance for other purposes, check the insurance section in this book for a discussion of those needs.

- Many individuals purchase plans that not only provide for the funeral, they also choose their caskets and plan their funeral in advance. These plans are also available through local mortuaries.

- Because of the extreme cost of funerals and burials, many people are now opting for cremation, whose cost is generally much less than that of a funeral. It was recently reported that cremations are now used in approximately fifty percent of deaths.

- Sometimes family members spend extraordinary amounts for a funeral because of the lack of attention showed to the deceased during the lifetime. A fancy funeral will not bring back missed relationships. Visit family members as often as possible. A contact by phone, email or postal mail is good if necessary, but a personal visit is best.

I, for one, am of the old school. I don't plan to get a burial plot or casket before I die, and I don't want to be cremated, because it may be plenty hot where I'm going anyway. So although I haven't planned for anything, I know the family will get rid of me in some way.

NOTES TO SELF

WRITE YOUR HISTORY

No one reaches retirement age without having fought a lot of battles. We win some, we lose some. Hopefully we win more than we lose. This process is what makes up life. It teaches and sets our priorities, our goals, our values; it measures our successes and failures and defines our relationships. Each person has traveled a different road and has a unique story to tell.

My grandfather, in his history, tells of moving their log home. They cut the house in half with a saw and dragged it with a team of forty horses, one-half at a time. My father's history tells of living in a dugout in the side of a mountain one winter during the Great Depression. These and many other facts about their lives would have been lost without a written history. During your retirement years, take the opportunity to write your history. It will be of great benefit to your children and future generations. Your history does not have to be long, complicated or even typed. Here are some suggestions that may help you to write your history:

- Write about periods of time, such as school years or college years.
- Write about events, such as births, marriages, deaths, moving or vocational changes.
- Be specific on names and dates of events.
- Tell of great or exciting events.
- Tell of disappointing or unhappy events.
- Describe people, places or things.
- Include your parents, children and grandchildren.
- Make a copy and give it to each of your children.

Future generations will be amazed and motivated by events in your life which you may feel of little consequence. Do not be discouraged or embarrassed about the story—it is your life, you lived it, it is unique.

NOTES TO SELF

_____

_____

CHAPTER NINE

QUALITY OF LIFE

WINNING THE RACE

I am convinced that one of the most difficult challenges you will face in this race of life is growing old gracefully, and because of the complexity of aging, few are able to do it gracefully. The aging process is one that gives little control to the recipient. Sometimes changes in health come very quickly, and we have little control over the consequences. Yet I do believe that many things over which we do have control can enhance our quality of life in spite of the many challenges that will, and do, come as we mature. It is in these retirement years when we determine how well we have run this race.

DON'T STOP

Many have the mistaken belief that when you reach age sixty -five it's all over. I'm there, I can retire, do nothing and be happy until I die. This does not have to be the case senaario for you, or for anyone else for that matter. At age sixty-five you may just be getting up your steam, you may be in your prime, you may just be getting started.

Consider Harland Sanders, who at age sixty-five was forced into retirement and only had a $105 Social Security check to live on. Unhappy with the idea, and unwilling to settle for what was proferred him, he set out on a business venture that made him one of the most recognized people in the world. Colonel Harland Sanders, the founder of Kentuckey Fried Chicken®, didn't stop at age sixty-five and you don't have to stop either. If you have an idea, goal or dream then age sixty-five is an excellent age to go for it. People who reach retirement age have more knowledge and experience, thus they have a better opportunity to succeed. Being active in persuit of a new business venture will help keep you young and healthy.

NOTES TO SELF

BE HAPPY

We all know individuals like Ebenezer Scrooge from Charles Dickens *A Christmas Carol*. These individuals spread doom and gloom wherever they go. No one likes to visit them, and no one likes to be in the presence of such individuals. We avoid them like the plague. I don't believe people of this type just get up in the morning and say, "I'm going to be mean, nasty and ugly today." Usually this type of personality is the result of a lot of unconscious reactions to things that happen to them in life. I believe people who always seem to be happy may be happy as a result of their unconscious reactions. If we become a happy or miserable person by unconscious reactions to circumstances, I also believe we can, by making conscious decisions, choose to be happy or miserable people. The choice is ours.

My friend Clyde always lifted me when I was in his presence. I always felt better when we parted than when I first went to visit him. It wasn't that Clyde didn't have reason to be miserable. He became a quadriplegic in his early twenties as a result of an accident. In the ensuing years he had many medical problems. Clyde had the perfect excuse to sit around in life being miserable and make everyone around him miserable. He chose not to do so. He married his childhood sweetheart, raised a family, gained an education, became a successful businessman and taught college—all from the confines of his wheelchair. He has outlived his life expectancy several times and is still going. Clyde knew he could be happy or he could be miserable. He chose to be happy, and people enjoy being in his presence.

If you don't know whether you are a happy or a unhappy person, I suggest you ask for an honest opinion from your spouse or close family members. If you don't like the answer, then know that you can change to the type of person you want to be. William James said, "The greatest discovery of any generation is that a human being can alter his life by altering his attitude." Many places offer help to change your attitude. Two places I use often and recommend are:

- The local library. You can check out many books on attitude that will help you become a happier person.
- The local bookstore, where you could spend an afternoon. There are hundreds of books on attitude. Purchase one or two you like, and if you do as I do, mark it up as you read.

Being happy may well be an art form. I believe that if you practice and work on being happy, your life will be much richer, and so will the lives of those people you associate with. My final advice on being happy would be to learn to *laugh at yourself*. We all make mistakes; we all do stupid things once in a while. When you realize you have done something stupid, you have two courses of action. First, you can get upset, rant and rave and generally make life miserable for yourself and all those around you. Second, you can recognize that you did something stupid and laugh at yourself, and laugh with others who are laughing at you. This second choice of laughing at yourself will ease the stress, make you happier, and make everyone else happier. Life is short. Be happy.

NOTES TO SELF

PLOM

It is easy to be consumed by our trials as we mature. It may be health or finances; it may be children or the weather. Whatever the problem, it may grow to consume all our time, thoughts and energy. This is what a friend of mine calls a PLOM Attack (Poor Little Ol' Me). If you find yourself with this type of a syndrome, the best way to solve it is to look around and find someone with bigger problems than you. Once you find people with bigger problems, yours might not seem so bad. You might be happy that your problems are all you have. So get on with living. Life is short. Enjoy it while you can.

NOTES TO SELF

ANGER AND GRUDGES

Years ago, a client of mine lost some money in a business venture. It just didn't work out. Rather than take his loss and move on with his life, he became consumed by the thought of getting even with his former business partner. He became so consumed with such thoughts that he wasted several years and many thousands of dollars. He literally lost three to four years of his life because rather than moving ahead, progressing, growing, learning and earning, he just wallowed in his PLOM syndrome. Life is short. We do not have time to be angry and hold grudges against family or fellow beings.

Many years ago, a little boy broke out the windows of his dad's car with a hammer. The father in anger pounded the little boy's hands with the hammer. Such a loss of self control should not be endured in the human race. If you find you have a problem in these areas, seek religious and professional counseling.

Several years ago, I read of two brothers who had an argument and stopped talking to one another. They lived in the same house for many years and failed to speak to each other. How sad it would be to write in your history that you spent your life hating someone or holding a grudge when life could be filled with happiness and accomplishment. Another client of mine lived next to his neighbor for forty years; they had a common driveway down a dirt lane for several hundred feet. Because of a disagreement they quit talking to each other and put a fence down the middle of the driveway in protest against each other. Many grudges are founded on items that have no value, things that are insignificant and emotions that are out of control. For those who have these challenges, I recommend you go to church, learn of God, and learn forgiveness.

NOTES TO SELF

EXERCISE

I have watched, with a great deal of interest, the part exercise plays in the quality of life. Numerous studies show that those who exercise regularly are happier, they live longer, and they are healthier. The statistics on exercise are in. Without question, those who exercise regularly have a better quality of life in spite of other challenges they may encounter. An example is my friend Darle.

Darle, at ninety years of age, does water aerobics three to four times a week, even when she doesn't feel much like going. She could let her chronic fatigue syndrome, her chronic bronchitis, her hip replacement or her age be an excuse, but she does not. I am thoroughly convinced that she is still alive and healthy because of her exercise (her positive attitude helps).

Being a couch potato and watching soaps is not an exercise. There are many forms of exercise, and many mature people use them regularly to improve their quality of life.

- walking
- running/jogging
- swimming
- water aerobics
- aerobics
- pilates
- tennis

- golf
- badminton
- mountain climbing
- mountain biking
- biking
- racquetball
- bowling
- rock climbing
- canoeing
- skiing
- snow boarding
- scuba diving
- hang gliding
- parasailing
- weight lifting
- tread mill
- fitness center
- Yoga

You can do unlimited things to give you physical exercise. Choose one or two or five you want to do, and do them regularly. You will be healthier and happier and live longer. And people will enjoy being around you.

I have watched in amazement as many people give up their physical abilities, such as walking or exercising, because it hurt. I have noted that whenever we give up any physical ability for a short period of time, we never regain it without a lot more pain and suffering. *Don't give up any physical ability*! (Still, I always got frustrated hitting a ball into the rough, losing it, finding it and hitting it back into the rough again.)

NOTES TO SELF

_____

_____

GET UP EARLY AND STAY UP LATE

When I was a kid, I never had trouble getting up early in the morning to go fishing or hunting. Now I never get up gracefully unless I have a specific reason to do so. It seems that many retired people wake up very early in the morning and lie in bed and worry about their problems. Because they go to bed early, they wake up early, and by evening they are exhausted and so go to bed early worrying about their problems. If you know someone or find yourself with this time schedule and worrying routine, I suggest several things you can do to improve your quality of life.

- When you wake up, whether at 3:00 a.m. or 6:00 a.m. get up and do something you are interested in.

- If you have a problem you are consistently worried about,

do something about it. Work at solving the problem. If you can't solve the problem, quit worrying about it; move on to something else.

- Stay up later doing something that holds your interest. (See other sections of this book for examples.) You will sleep better and feel better.

NOTES TO SELF

_____

_____

GOALS

Goals are the lifeblood of accomplishment; nothing has ever been accomplished without goals. Everyone should have goals. The measure of what we achieve is based on the goals we have. Our goal may be as simple as getting out of bed in the morning, or as large as planning a trip around the world. Whatever your goals, hang on to them and pursue them. My purpose in bringing up this subject is to encourage you to enlarge your goals. Somewhere between getting out of bed in the morning and planning a trip around the world there have got to be some goals that fit your wants and needs.

Is there anything in your life you have always wanted to do but never got around to it? Something you wanted to see, some place you wanted to go, a book you wanted to read or a book you wanted to write, someone you wanted to visit, or a business you wanted to start, a degree you wanted to get, or a subject you wanted to study, a mountain you wanted to climb or a seabed you wanted to examine, a slope you wanted to ski or a course you wanted to golf? Whatever it is you want to do, set it as a goal and pursue it. My father, though suffering from terminal cancer, asked his doctor if he could pursue a particular goal. The doctor told him he might die while he is doing it. My father said, "I might die whether I do it or not." So he pursued his goal, accomplished it successfully, and lived several years after. How sad it would have been to have never pursued the goal and never had the satisfaction of accomplishment.

May I suggest you make important goals—only important goals will motivate you to get out of bed in the morning. Involve other people in your goals. Tell your family and friends of your goals; let them be a part of the planning and the success. Winona graduated from college at the age of eighty-two, much to the delight of family and friends. What are your goals?

NOTES TO SELF

_____

_____

GOOD BOOKS

Over the years my wife has learned one valuable lesson: when I am in the middle of a good book, the only way to get my attention is to look me right in the eye. Nothing can capture one's total attention and imagination as well as a good book. May I recommend that part of your retirement itinerary be a regular trip to the library or bookstore for a good book. Many of the good movies you enjoy come from books. I believe your life will be richer and more enjoyable if you continue to read. I also believe you will not become such a boring person if you continue to read.

I have found some favorite books I would like to recommend. Carl Sandburg's four-volume set on Abraham Lincoln, Harcourt, Brace & Company, NY, 1939;. Hinckley, Gordon B., *Standing For Something,* Times Books, a division of Random House, Inc., NY, 2000 (Foreword by Mike Wallace); J. K. Rowling, *Harry Potter Series*, Arthur A. Levin Books, 1997; *National Geographic* magazines, Official Journal of the National Geographic Society; Bradley, James, *Flags of Our Fathers, Hero's of Iwo Jima,* Bantam, NY, 2000; J. R. R. Tolkien, *The Lord of the Rings Series,* Houghton Mifflin Company, Boston and NY, 1994; Sachar, Louis, *Holes,* Frances Foster Books, Farrar, Straus and Giroux, NY, 1998; Burnett, Frances Hodgson, *The Secret Garden*, Harper Collins Publishers, New York, NY, 1911; Timberlake, Lewis, Reed, Marietta, *Born to Win,* Tyndale House Publishers, Inc. Weaton, IL, 1986; Langguth, A.J. *Patriots, The Men Who Started the American Revolution,* A Touchstone Book, Simon and Schuster, New York, NY, 1988.

There are many, many good books, but there are also some bad ones. Choose some good ones and try a variety of subjects, such as mysteries, love stories, biographies, histories, geography, travel—any number of things you want to read about, fiction and fact. There is nothing like a good book to take you away from worrying about the challenges of maturing. You can get good books at your local library, at any number of bookstores, and on the Internet. If all else fails, borrow one from a friend.

NOTES TO SELF

GOOD MOVIES

I have always loved good movies. Now what is good to me may not be good to you. I believe a good movie is one that doesn't exploit sex or violence or insult human dignity. With the advent of television, many in our society have quit viewing quality programs.

However, the TV, the VCR and the DVD have enabled us to bring into our homes some of the best movie entertainment available. You can pick movies up at the library or buy them and view them whenever you want. I recommend you get a DVD player and become associated with some video/DVD rental and sales businesses and lose yourself in the thousands of good movies available. The local library in my town has one of the finest collections of videos and DVD's in the area. I like to watch John Wayne and Cary Grant movies, and they cost me only $1.00 pcr week.

Many of my mature clients have been very lonely over the years. No one comes to visit them, and when they do they don't stay long. The many hours of loneliness and boredom can be relieved by a video or DVD. The cost of video and DVD players varies widely. You can get one for $50 to $60. There are more expensive ones, but I have found the inexpensive do just fine. When one breaks down, I throw it away and get a new one.

NOTES TO SELF

_____

_____

GOOD TELEVISION

Many of my clients spend a great deal of time watching TV. This is personal, but I don't think there is much good on regular TV today. The regular viewing channels are filled with sexual innuendo, degrading subject matter, and slapstick comedy. There are, if you choose, much better things to watch on your TV. You can access many channels through cable or dish which will open the world to your TV viewing. I recommend you get away from the soap operas, the slapstick comedy and the sexually explicit talk shows and spend your time in some of the following areas:
- The History Channel

- Travel channels
- The Discovery Channel
- Old movie channels
- Science and nature channels
- Weather channels
- C-Span

I don't even like to watch the news, because most of it is so negative. I get my news on the Internet—I am always up-to-date, I always know what is going on, and I can select the quality of news I watch or read.

Some 200 different channels are available to you. Choose the good ones. They will make your life richer, you will be happier, and you won't spend the time in retirement staring at the fireplace, waiting for someone to visit.

NOTES TO SELF

_____

_____

GOOD MUSIC

As a boy in junior high school, I sang in a boy's choir. In high school I sang in an a capella choir. After marriage, I sang in the church choir. I have been singing for many years, and I love good music. Much can be gained by music—it lifts our souls and gladdens our hearts. Music can be instrumental or vocal; it can be a single performer or an entire choir, orchestra or band. You can sing with it, hum along with it, or tap your foot to it. It can be motivational, inspirational, patriotic or just relaxing. I believe everyone should have good music in their lives, especially during retirement.

When you retire you will find a lot of time on your hands. Some people manage to keep their days full, but some lose their zest for life, and spend much time sitting and worrying. Music can help set a tone in your home that will enable you to be happier, healthier, and more active and help you endure the challenges of maturing. You don't have to be retired to receive the benefits of good music in your home. As my wife and I raised our children, we helped establish the home environment by the use of good music. We always played the music we wanted to influence our children. Even today, when most of the children are gone, we continue that practice. We have a CD player that holds 51 CDs. In it we have a very broad selection of good music. We play these CDs at a low volume during all our waking hours. It sets the tone and mood of our home.

There is good music in our society and there is bad music in our society. I believe you should stay away from music that is loud, erratic, or boisterous, has bad lyrics, combines immoral innuendos or teachings, and is performed by poorly dressed and partially clad performers. There is much good in music, and I recommend that it become a part of your life—not only in retirement, not only while raising a family, but from the time you are old enough to recognize and participate in good music.

NOTES TO SELF

_____

_____

KEEP YOUR MIND BUSY

Many years ago, while talking with Dr. John Bowen, a friend, he made a statement I have thought about a great deal over the ensuing years. He said, "Senility is sometimes brought on by laziness of the mind." In my many years of meeting with mature people, I have witnessed the ageing process and believe Doctor John was right. Many times after retirement, individuals just quit using their brains. Sitting in a chair, staring out the window, watching a soap opera, or lying in bed worrying does not keep the mind active and growing. We get in ruts and go over the same things time and time again. Therefore, I recommend with all of the enthusiasm I can muster that you get involved in living, in growing, in learning, in serving and keeping your mind busy in good things.

This subject of keeping your mind busy is what this section of the book is all about: education, travel, goals, good books, music and movies. It is about exercise, being happy, lifting others, service, love and religion. This section is about quality of life. Many times over the years I have visited with elderly people who have given up on life. They have no goals, they have no friends, they have no desires, and they just wait to die. A lady in Cleveland, Ohio, in her fifties said, "I just want to die. I have lived in this home for eleven years and I don't know who lives on either side of me. I just want to die." By following the recommendations in this book, you not only can improve the quality of life to the point that it is worth living, you can also lift and improve the quality of life of those around you.

I believe that challenges are a sign of life. We all have challenges. I also believe that the quality of our life is a result of how we respond to those challenges. When we get to thinking that our challenges are beyond our capacity to deal with them, let us look around. We will find many with greater challenges. If you were allowed to trade challenges, you would probably select the ones you already have because you can deal with them. May I suggest again that you spend your time in retirement in trying to lift those who have challenges bigger than your challenges.

This week, Maude died. Her funeral is tomorrow. She was eighty-eight years old and spent many of her remaining years helping other people. In her early eighties she delivered meals to others who needed the help, even though many of those she served were younger than she. When they needed to go to the doctor, she drove them. She took them shopping, to appointments, to lunch or to performances. She wore out her life in the service of others. Her passing is not mourning, but a celebration of a great person who has served and lifted others. This is what quality of life is all about. I hope your life is as rich as hers was, and that when you depart to the next life, those you have served and lifted will call you blessed because of how you spent your retirement years.

NOTES TO SELF

_____

_____

RELIGION

Some may not believe that religion has anything to do with estate planning or even retirement. I disagree with that thought. I have, over the years, become acquainted with many people who were deeply religious. They represented many different religious beliefs. At the same time I have known many who have little or no place for religion in their lives. It is my observation that those who have a belief in the divine nature of man and in a superior being have a better quality of life. They are more content with life, are happier, and have a sense of peace and a respect for others, and a respect for sacred things.

I believe that as you go into retirement, you should be active in a religion of your choice. I do not care what religion you choose—that is up to you; but be active in and embrace your religion. Live what you believe. This will give you peace of mind and comfort during the declining years of your life.

I do not emphasize any particular religion. You may be Catholic, Jewish, Baptist, Methodist, Moslem or any other religion. I myself am a member of The Church of Jesus Christ of Latter-day Saints; there are very good people in all religions. The point is this: people who have a religious belief, who are active in their religion and live what they believe, are more content in retirement. They are helpful to others, they serve others, they handle the stress of maturing better, and they have a better quality of life during retirement. Religions teach moral values which are the basis for all good things that survive in society. Without moral values, society would degenerate to a system of survival of the fittest and dog-eat-dog. Religious moral values teach love, compassion, understanding and service to our fellow beings. Without the religious values of our forefathers, our nation would not have achieved the greatness we benefit from today.

Religion is an important aspect of retirement. Be involved!

NOTES TO SELF

_____

_____

SERVICE

Several years ago I asked a client how he was dealing with retirement. He said he didn't know how he ever had time to work because he was so busy now. I pursued the question: "What is keeping you so busy?" He said, "Shoveling the snow for all the old people in the neighborhood." I said, "It only snows in the winter. What do you do the rest of the year?" His comment was, "I mow lawns, I fix things in houses, I take people shopping—I don't know how I had time to work."

Recently a friend's grandfather died at age ninety-three. Before his death a relative offered to take him shopping. He gracefully declined because the kid next door always took him shopping. It was later revealed that the "kid next door" was seventy-five years young. What a great way to spend retirement—helping others. In our society, many people spend a great deal of time serving others. They bless the lives of those around them, many times without anyone knowing of their service. When it comes to quality of life in retirement, we find it changes, sometimes without warning. As we age, we may find we have needs that other people can help us with. It is extremely important that we learn to receive service from others in a graceful manner. We do not need to apologize for our conditions, but we should learn to say "Thank You!" in a gracious manner to those who serve us.

The old saying "What goes around, comes around" is true, particularly when it comes to service and being served. While you can, look for opportunities to help those who need help. These opportunities are all about us. Remember, at some point in time you also may need to be served. Some suggestions for service are as follows:

- grandparent at an elementary school.
- pink lady at the hospital
- serving food at the homeless shelter
- reading stories to children at the library
- serving in the Boy Scouts and Girl Scouts
- visiting rest homes
- community action programs
- food drives
- clothing drives
- tutoring students
- driving elderly people
- serving in relief organizations

This list could go on and on. It is as long as your imagination. Find a reason to serve and a cause that will motivate you to get out of the house and do something for someone else.

NOTES TO SELF

TRAVEL

When it comes to improving the quality of our life, one of the most rewarding experiences is travel. The number of places to go and places to see is endless. The first time I visited the Niagara Falls, I was captivated by the sheer energy and magnitude of what lay before me. I have returned to the falls on many occasions, and the joy I experienced on my first visit has never diminished in subsequent visits. An aunt had never traveled more than a few miles from her home. Many years ago we had an opportunity to take her to the Northwest. Her sheer joy at seeing the Pacific Ocean was worth the entire trip.

One year we visited the Pacific and the Atlantic Oceans. We walked the Boardwalk in New Jersey, visited the Mammoth Caves in Kentucky and the Lehman Caves in Nevada. We saw the Great Lakes and the Mississippi River, Mount Rushmore and the Badlands. On other occasions we visited New York, the Redwoods, San Francisco, Sea World in San Diego, and the Space Needle in Seattle. The list could go on and on, but it is not about where I have visited, it is about where *you* could go and what *you* could see.

More important about travel is not necessarily the things you see but the people you meet and the people you take with you. I love, in September of the year, to get in the car and drive the back roads of the country. I take time to stop and look and visit with many wonderful people who live in our society. You will find that many are just like you and have had the same trials and challenges. They can be lifted by your visiting with them, just as you can be lifted by taking time to visit.

Travel can be an expensive item, if you let it. However, there are some things you can do to travel at a minimal expense, within your budget.

- Shop for low travel fares on the Internet (air, bus, Amtrak, cruise, etc.).
- Sleep in your car, van, SUV or a borrowed motor home.
- Get a motel every second or third night.
- Fix meals rather than go to restaurants.
- Take someone with you to share expenses.
- Take someone with you whom you enjoy being with.
- Stay at relatives and eat their food.
- Travel in the off season.
- Avoid tourist traps.
- Obtain annual National Park Passes.
- Get a "Golden Age" pass from the National Parks Service. It is $10.00 for the rest of your life.
- Drive a fuel-economy vehicle (more miles per gallon).

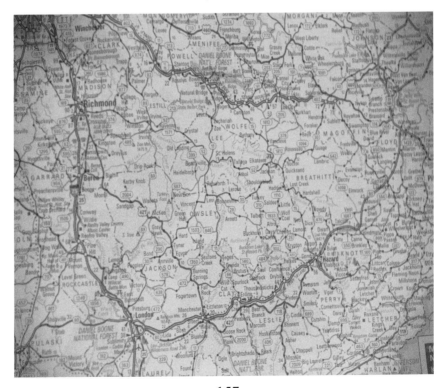

Retirement is a time all people look forward to, when they can enjoy the benefits of their life's labors and do the things they always wanted to do. For many, retirement is a time when their health is gone, their wealth is gone, and their desire is gone. In many instances the children are gone or we lose a spouse. When confronted with these circumstances, there are many groups with whom one can travel during retirement, such as church groups and senior citizen groups.

Travel is something that can be pursued when you are young or when you have a family to enjoy it with. But if you have not taken the opportunity to travel previously in your life, start now and pursue it with vigor, whatever your age.

NOTES TO SELF

_____

_____

CONCLUSION

Retirement is not a tree standing on a hillside by itself. It is a tree in a forest surrounded by many trees whose roots and branches intertwine. They hold up and support each other to produce a complete grove that can stand as a unit, independent of what goes on around it. Each subject of discussion in this book has been an essential part of a retirement plan. Failure to complete any particular aspect of the retirement plan may result in an incomplete retirement. True, many things can go wrong in retirement. But with all the trees in place, many things can go right.

The chapters in this book speak for themselves. They define the race of life. Each gives you guidelines and directions for items you should consider. Each is essential, but you are the only one who can push your retirement plan through to completion. The attorney can complete Trust documents, but he or she doesn't generally do taxes. Your CPA is skilled at taxes, but he or she doesn't have the ability to foster personal relationships. Your financial advisor is interested in investments, but not in health and exercise. Only you have the ability and desire or interest to make sure it all comes together.

This book has been designed to make you aware of the many facets to consider in your race. Your notes on items that are important to you can be an excellent guide while you work with your professionals.

Some have a long time before retirement, others very little. Many have retirement in place. Congratulations! Wherever you are, use the time you have to make the best retirement you can. Develop a plan and pursue it relentlessly. Don't quit! If you stumble, get up and push forward. Keep your eye on the goal and don't be distracted. Success is within your grasp.

I wish you success and good luck in achieving the retirement you desire!

REFERENCES

1   Equity Services Hotline, December, 2004, p. 4.

2   Fidelity Investments, Smart Move, *Which IRA Works for You*, p. 1.

3   Focus On, *Retirement Plan Distributions*, Emerald Publications, 1996, pp. 6, 16

4   Fannie Mae, *Considering a Reverse Mortgage*, 2004.

5   Fannie Mae, *Home Equity Conversion Mortgage (HECM)*, Consumer Fact Sheet, August, 2004.

6   IRS Form 706 Instructions.

7   Instructions for form 709, United States Gift (and Generation-Skipping Transfer) Tax Return.   Department of the Treasury, Internal Revenue Service, 2004.

8   Social Security Handbook, Social Security Online, www.socialsecurity.gov, Sec. 128.2.

WINNING OR LOSING

The information contained in this book is of such importance that it needs to be shared with Family and Friends. Additional copies may be obtained by visiting our website at: **winningorlosing.com**, or the publishers website at: **deverepublishing.com**. If you prefer you may also send the following order form directly to the publisher.

ORDER FORM

Please send me _____ copies of **WINNING OR LOSING** at the price of $24.95 each and no charge for shipping and handling (Utah residence include $1.60 state sales tax). My check or money order for $_____ is enclosed made payable to Devere Publishing.

Name_____

Address_____

City/State/Zip_____

Phone(____) _____   Fax(___) _____

E-mail_____

Send order to: Devere Publishing Inc.
                  P O Box 970965
                  Orem, UT 84097-0965

                  Please allow 15 days for delivery

Additional copies may also be obtained at your local bookstore.

INDEX